Masterpieces from the House of

FABERGÉ

Masterpieces from the House of
FABERGÉ

Alexander von Solodkoff
with essays by
Roy D. R. Betteley, Paul Schaffer,
A. Kenneth Snowman, and Marilyn Pfeifer Swezey
Edited by Christopher Forbes

ФАБЕРЖЕ
С.ПЕТЕРБУРГЪ
МОСКВА, ОДЕССА
КІЕВЪ, ЛОНДОНЪ

Harry N. Abrams, Inc., Publishers, New York

Title page: Imperial Presentation Frame of gold, presented by Czar Alexander III to his wife, Marie Feodorovna, whose monogram decorates it. Photograph of Czar Nicholas II in uniform of the Life Guard Hussars.

"Fabergé: Vous êtes un génie incomparable"

The Dowager Empress Marie Feodorovna
Easter, 1914

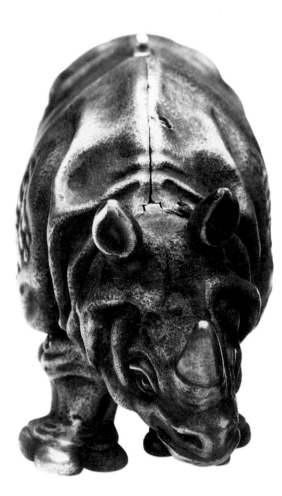

Project Director: Darlene Geis
Designer: Darilyn Lowe

Library of Congress Cataloging in Publication Data

Solodkoff, A. von
  Masterpieces from the House of Fabergé.

  Bibliography: p.
  1. Faberzhe (Firm)   2. Easter eggs—Russian S.F.S.R.
3. Goldwork—Russian S.F.S.R.   4. Jewelry—Russian
S.F.S.R.   I. Forbes, Christopher.   II. Faberzhe (Firm)
III. Title
NK7398.F33S65   1984   739.2'092'4   84-2779
ISBN 0-8109-0933-2

Copyright © 1984 Harry N. Abrams, Inc. and FORBES Inc.
Copyright © 1984 Roy D.R. Betteley, "Fabergé in Thailand"
Copyright © 1984 Paul Schaffer, "A La Vieille Russie's Fabergé"
Copyright © 1984 A. Kenneth Snowman, "Wartski and Fabergé"

All Fabergé works illustrated are from the FORBES Magazine Collection
unless otherwise indicated.

Published in 1984 by Harry N. Abrams, Incorporated, New York
All rights reserved. No part of the contents of this book may be
reproduced without the written permission of the copyright holders.

Printed and bound in Japan

Contents

On Collecting Fabergé

Any collection is a living thing as long as its collectors are. We are, and so the FORBES Magazine Collection of Fabergé is never long static.

Since I wrote the Foreword below to Hermione Waterfield's book on the subject, published over a decade ago, 159 Fabergé pieces have been added up to this moment. Twelve objects have been "deaccessioned," usually in the process of upgrading the collection.

The crown jewels, of course, of this greatest artist of *objets d'art* are the Imperial Easter Eggs. In the past decades we've added five to the first five in the collection. The FORBES ten equal in number those under Communist eye in the Kremlin Armory Museum. We aim one of these days to pull ahead.

The 300 year old Romanov dynasty came to an abrupt end on July 16, 1918, when the Czar Nicholas II, his wife, and five children were murdered in the cellar of a Siberian house during one of the bloodiest wars of all time. Not too many months after the governmental chaos that followed, Russia became the modern world's first Communist state.

When very young I read with horrified fascination an abundantly illustrated volume on World War I. Its chapter about the Russian Revolution and the massacre of the Romanov family included a picture of a Fabergé Imperial Egg to illustrate the pre-War extravagance of Russia's rulers.

In London many years later (but still longer ago than I like to remember), I bought my wife a Fabergé cigarette box for Christmas. Before we met and married, she too had been fascinated by Fabergé's fabulous combination of fantasy and artistry. The first acquisition was exciting for us both. Since then she has treasured and constantly used it—until I "borrowed" it to be part of our permanent Fabergé exhibition in the lobby of the FORBES Magazine Building.

Our second personal Fabergé piece came a couple of years later when I presented her with a wee charm-bracelet-size egg of white enamel with an enameled red cross. This too has been "borrowed" and is now also on display at FORBES.

Our first major acquisition was the Duchess of Marlborough

Opposite: The top of Malcolm Forbes's desk with Fabergé pieces in daily use, among them the Imperial Writing Portfolio bearing the crowned double monogram of Nicholas and Alexandra.

Gold Imperial Presentation Cigarette Case, by Niukkanen. Collection of Mrs. Malcolm S. Forbes.

Egg. It cost us three and a half times the estimate, and I was torn between the thrill of having it and a sinking feeling that perhaps we had overbid as a result of auction fever.

Reassurance was swift, though, when the late Alexander Schaffer, founder of Fifth Avenue's A La Vieille Russie, identified himself as the underbidder and invited me to view the major Fabergé masterpieces in his safe. . . .

Fortunately, from the pocketbook point of view, I have never been too much turned on by Fabergé's animals nor, with a few exceptions, his flowers. There was only one animal in the extensive Lansdell K. Christie Collection that I was anxious to have—the Crystal Polar Bear. . . . The [current] Aga Khan bought all the others and, as a result, has one of the greatest Fabergé zoos in the world. . . .

Those who know most about these matters tell us that our collection is now worth many times what it cost. As the son of a canny Scotsman, I like to believe it so.

But I hope we never have to find out.

Malcolm S Forbes

Hunting for Easter Eggs

The fatal fantasies of a doomed dynasty or the ultimate expressions of the art of the goldsmith and the jeweler—or both? Fabergé Easter eggs have, since their creation, exerted an appeal far beyond their intrinsic worth in gold and precious stones.

From the time of the first public exhibitions in the early part of this century, connoisseurs and the general public alike have been enthralled by the whimsy and craftsmanship of these sumptuous objects. After the brutal murder of Nicholas II and his family, an element of tragedy and romance further heightened public fascination in these creations so intimately associated with the ill-fated Czar.

With the Communist takeover on November 7, 1918, and Peter Carl Fabergé's death in exile two years later, "Fabergé" ceased to be something bought and became instead something collected. A number of famous families and individuals associated with the history of Fabergé treasures were both consumers and collectors. Into this category fall King George V and his acquisitive consort, Queen Mary, Sir Harold and Lady Anastasia Werner—she was the great-granddaughter of Czar Nicholas I—and on the other side of the Atlantic, Baltimorean Henry Walters, who shopped at Fabergé when he visited St. Petersburg aboard his yacht the *Narada* in 1900 and thirty years later acquired two Imperial Easter Eggs for the museum which he ultimately gave to his native city.

In addition to the numerous Fabergé *objets* which left Russia in the hands of emigrés such as the Youssoupoffs and the Nobels, the greatest Fabergé treasures, including many of the Imperial Easter Eggs, were actually exported by the Communist government during the mid-1920s to earn Western currency. The chief intermediary in this exchange of culture for cash was Dr. Armand Hammer, aided by his brother Victor, who had studied art history at Princeton University. Dr. Hammer not only brought incalculable quantities of Russian artworks to America, but he also created a broadly based appreciation and market for them—at the height of the Great Depression. John

Her Majesty Queen Sirikit of Thailand, visiting New York in 1980, is shown the Lilies of the Valley Egg and Coronation Egg by Christopher Forbes.

Walker, the former director of the National Gallery, describes it in his book *Self Portrait with Donors*:

> When the stock market collapsed, the art market disintegrated. . . . As his brothers in New York despairingly pointed out, their Fabergé Easter Eggs were beautiful but not edible. . . . Undismayed . . . [Hammer] wrote to a dozen of the leading department stores in various cities asking for an entire floor to exhibit his unique collection of what he claimed were the greatest works of art ever to leave Russia. . . . Only one favorable reply was received . . . from Scruggs Vandervoort . . . in St. Louis. . . . He went to each newspaper. . . . He made the Hammer Collection news. . . . When the exhibition opened, there were a thousand people waiting to get in. . . . Marshall Field and Company . . . in Chicago . . . was an even greater triumph. . . . They wound up at Lord and Taylor's in New York, where they had their greatest triumph of all.

Many of America's most renowned collectors of Fabergé first learned about the "Goldsmith to the Last Czars" from Dr. Hammer's traveling exhibition. These included Matilda Geddings Gray, whose three Imperial Easter Eggs are now on loan to the New Orleans Museum; India Minshall, whose collection, including one Imperial Easter Egg, now belongs to the Cleveland Museum; and most spectacularly of all, the unassuming Lillian Thomas Pratt. Her Fabergé hoard was kept in shoe boxes, and upon her death in 1947 was delivered to the Virginia Museum in the back of a station wagon. Among the almost two hundred pieces which thus arrived in Richmond were five Imperial Easter Eggs.

Other collectors who developed a taste for Fabergé—kindness of Dr. Hammer—were Jack and Belle Linsky. What began with a cigarette box soon grew into a collection which in Mrs. Linsky's own words, quoted in *Connoisseur* magazine, was "the second greatest—next to the English Queen's."

In the same interview, Gary Graffman continues the tale:

> The neophyte collectors were embarrassed, however, when their friend the late James Rorimer, director of the Met from 1955 to 1966, belittled their turn-of-the-century trinkets as a waste of money and of their collecting energies. They promptly sold most of the pieces. Shortly thereafter, the Fabergé revival began and, to Mrs. Linsky's fury, the same museum whose director had recently scorned her bibelots sponsored an exhibition in which many of the newly fashionable (and newly ex-Linsky) pieces were featured. Stung, Mrs. Linsky vowed, "Never again will I ask for or listen to any expert's advice!"

When many of Mrs. Linsky's Fabergé *objets* appeared, to her rightful annoyance, in a special gallery off the Great Hall of The Metropolitan Museum, it was as part of the collection of Lansdell Christie.

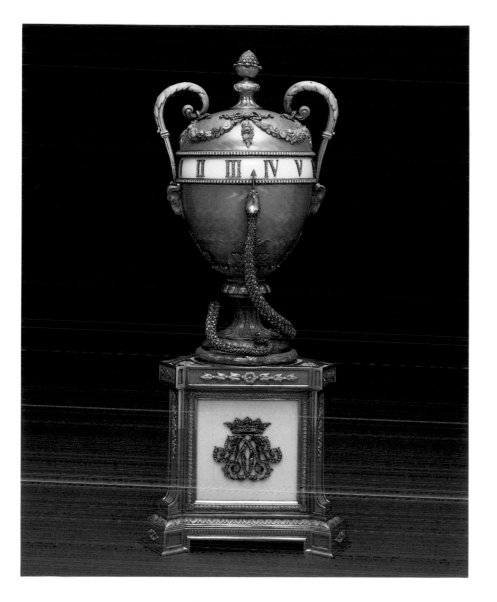

Duchess of Marlborough Egg, by Perchin. Purchased in 1902 in Russia by the Duchess, American-born heiress Consuelo Vanderbilt, it was later owned by Ganna Walska. In 1965 it became the first important piece of Fabergé in the FORBES Magazine Collection.

His three magnificent Easter eggs as well as more than two dozen other important pieces, many ex-Linsky, in turn formed the only en bloc acquisition by the FORBES Magazine Collection.

That collection, which now is rivaled only by the Kremlin's in the number of Imperial Easter Eggs, was conceived in the mid-1960s as a way of commemorating the fiftieth anniversary of the founding of FORBES by B. C. Forbes in September 1917—less than two months before the Bolsheviks seized power in Russia. The "egg hunt" began on Saturday, May 15, 1965, when the "Property of *Madame Ganna Walska* removed from 'Lotusland', Santa Barbara, California," was sold at public auction. Ganna Walska, a Polish-born soprano and would-be opera star, was profitably married in the 1920s to Harold Fowler McCormick, son of Chicago's "Reaper King." Among her *objets* falling under Parke-Bernet's hammer that afternoon was Lot 326: *Important wrought gold, rose and white enamel, serpent and egg ro-*

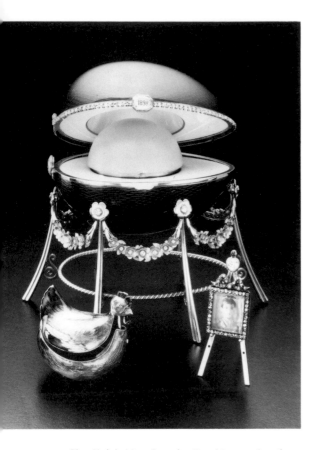

The Kelch Hen Egg, by Perchin, made of gold, strawberry-red and white enamel, diamonds, and rubies. The hinged yolk opens to reveal a hen which in turn contains a folding easel with a miniature of Czarevitch Alexis. Presented on Easter 1898 by Alexander Kelch to his wife, Barbara, whose portrait originally graced the easel. The gold stand was made for a later owner, King Farouk of Egypt.

tary clock, set with diamonds, by Carl Fabergé, Dated 1902. When bidding stopped at over four times the high estimate, underbidder Alexander Schaffer introduced himself to the purchaser, publisher Malcolm S. Forbes. Still bemused by his own boldness (or folly, as his Scottish-born father would have undoubtedly described it), Forbes could barely keep a straight face when Mr. Schaffer graciously suggested that, if Mr. Forbes were interested in *important* pieces of Fabergé, he might like to drop by A La Vieille Russie that afternoon. Although it had just set a new Fabergé auction record, Madame Ganna Walska's enameled gold egg set with diamonds and pearls (which later research proved to have been made for the Duchess of Marlborough, the former Consuelo Vanderbilt) did not, it was clear from Mr. Schaffer's careful emphasis on the word *important,* fall into that category. And perhaps it is not quite in the same league as the Renaissance Egg, the last of Fabergé's masterpieces created for Czar Alexander III, or the Orange Tree Egg, Czar Nicholas II's automated musical Easter surprise for his mother in 1911. These were among the treasures that Alexander Schaffer produced from his Ali Baba's cave of an office that afternoon. They quickly became the first and second in the fabled series of Imperial Easter Eggs to enter the FORBES Magazine Collection.

Several months later, one of the most important collections of Fabergé in the world came on the market. Assembled by shipping magnate Lansdell Christie, the collection had been exhibited at the Corcoran Gallery in Washington, D.C., before being placed on "permanent" loan to The Metropolitan Museum of Art in New York. Happily for FORBES, The Metropolitan was between directors and, there being no one to rally the funds necessary to keep these sumptuous and historic objects for the museum, Christie's estate turned to Alexander Schaffer to handle the disposition of the major pieces. Three more *important* Easter eggs, the Chanticleer Egg and the Spring Flowers Egg, as well as the almost edibly enameled Kelch Hen Egg, were thus gathered into the FORBES basket.

Next came perhaps one of the most poignant of all the pieces created by Fabergé for his imperial patrons: the egg presented by Nicholas to Alexandra in 1911 on the Easter following the fifteenth anniversary of their coronation. Flanking miniatures of the Czar, the Czarina, and their five children are nine additional tiny paintings of the major events of Nicholas II's reign. These incredible examples of the miniaturist's art, decorating an egg only 5⅛ inches high, are reproduced in enlarged format, and the events portrayed are chronicled fully, in Marilyn Swezey's essay farther on in this book.

Since this acquisition, five more eggs from the matchless series created by Fabergé for the Imperial Family have joined the FORBES Magazine Collection. These include the so-called First Imperial Egg, the Resurrection Egg, and the Cross of St. George Egg. More modest than most of its predecessors, this last egg with its silver shell (a gesture to wartime austerity!) was the final Easter present to be delivered by Fabergé to the Imperial Family. In the spring of 1916, in a letter to Nicholas II, Dowager Empress Marie Feodorovna wrote:

> Christ has indeed arisen! I kiss you three times and thank you with all my heart for your dear cards and lovely egg with miniatures, which dear old Fabergé brought himself. It is beautiful. It is so sad not to be together. I wish you, my dear darling Nicky, with all my heart all the best things and success in everything.
>
> *— Your fondly loving old*
> Mama

The tragic irony of the Czarina's wishes for her son's "success in everything" would be only too sadly apparent a few short years later, with the Czar and his family bloodily murdered and she herself en route to exile, first in England and later in her native Denmark.

The egg was inherited by her daughter, Grand Duchess Xenia, who in turn bequeathed it to her son, Prince Vassily Romanov. FORBES missed its chance to buy this Fabergé egg in the early 1970s and had to wait until it had passed through several collections, including that of the internationally known perfume company of the same name, before it finally came to roost at 60 Fifth Avenue.

After several years of on-again-off-again discussions as delicate as any SALT treaty negotiations, my father was able to persuade Kenneth Snowman of Wartski in London to part with the two eggs purchased by his father in the USSR in 1927. The Coronation Egg is perhaps the single best known of Fabergé's fantasies, with its miniature golden carriage which took more than fifteen months to create. The Lilies of the Valley Egg is one of the firm's rare essays into the then contemporary Art Nouveau style.

Since there are still Imperial Eggs in private collections, as well as several unaccounted for, the chance of surpassing the Soviets in this delightfully irrelevant area remains a tantalizing prospect for a company that publishes a magazine known as "The Capitalist Tool."

The egg hunt continues.

Christopher Forbes

Miniature Reliquary in the Gothic Style, by Perchin, made of nephrite, gold, and white and red enamel. The miniature casket on the right, from the Kimbell Art Museum, Ft. Worth, Texas, dates from 1250–1300, Limoges, France, and is champlevé enamel on copper over wood.

History of the House of Fabergé

Alexander von Solodkoff

The subject of Fabergé remains universally fascinating, combining as it does a colorful period of history with glittering jewels, art and design with nostalgia, and for a final fillip, the still unsolved mystery of several missing treasures.

The present study has two main themes. First, to outline most of the original sources and the documentary material about Fabergé which has recently come to light, thus adding to the existing body of information. Here we find a letter from the Empress Marie Feodorovna, the correspondence of Fabergé's Moscow branch with the designer Oswald Jones, as well as references from Fabergé's catalogue of 1899 and his London stock books. As a result of these and other newly discovered facts, the dating of some of the imperial Easter Eggs, described in a chapter of their own, has been revised.

Secondly, these pages attempt to trace the collecting of Fabergé objects from the late nineteenth century until today, with especial emphasis on buying before the Russian Revolution and the beginning of modern collecting in the 1930s. The emphasis on collecting seems especially appropriate for a book illustrating objects from the FORBES Magazine Collection, the most important assemblage of Fabergé's works of art in the United States—if not in the world.

With regard to collecting jewelry and objects of vertu, one is bound to mention the *Wunderkammer* of the Renaissance, with which Fabergé's works seem to have great affinities and a knowledge of which helps to understand his distinctive style.

A sixteenth-century *Wunderkammer,* or *cabinet de curiosité,* was a collection of intrinsically precious works of art combined with ethnographica, zoological oddities, relics, and scientific instruments that were collected, above all, for their rarity. This hodgepodge of objects might well include a jewel by a famous goldsmith, the (alleged) horn of a unicorn, a stuffed crocodile, a gold-mounted bezoar, or an ancient Greek vase. Among the many princely collections of the sixteenth century, those belonging to Emperor Rudolph II in Prague, the Medici in Florence, and Archduke Ferdinand in Ambras became the most celebrated.

Right: Ice Pendant of rock crystal, platinum, and diamonds bought in 1913 for £60.

Below: A page from Fabergé's 1913 London sales ledger recording purchases by a Duke, a Duchess, a Baron, and an Oppenheim—the latter bought the Ice Pendant.

Wunderkammer objects could be classified within three categories: as being of naturalistic, antiquarian, or artistic interest. Comparing these criteria for a collection with the range of Fabergé's work, one can easily demonstrate parallels. For the naturalistic category, photographs show that some of his workshops assembled a gallery of mounted animals which were to be copied in miniature in hardstone or silver. Fabergé also carefully studied the natural qualities of hardstones—their shapes, colors, and structures—which were then integrated into the final creation of an object, giving it a special effect such as a tree-shaped detail, or in the case of moss-agate or speckled hardstone, suggesting the markings of an animal's fur. Fabergé even used actual rhinoceros horn or tiger claws for the decoration of his objects.

The antiquarian aspect of Fabergé's work is exemplified in a number of objects which incorporate already existing collectibles from other periods or foreign cultures. Eighteenth-century coins are frequently found in his pieces. Fabergé was also fascinated by Oriental art, especially that of Japan. His own urge to collect is demonstrated by his large group of netsuke, now in the Hermitage Museum in Leningrad. Objects incorporating antique Chinese snuff bottles or carved Indian jades, which were given Fabergé mounts, are examples of his strong art-historical interest.

The artistic aspect of Fabergé's work needs no justification. His workshops were among the last ever to produce objects of unsurpassed artistic and technical perfection. His mastery can be seen in the high quality of the varied designs and means of decoration of objects that were never repeated or mass-produced. Technical curiosities such as his automatic mechanisms seem to follow in a direct line from the marvels of the *Wunderkammer* collections.

A final noteworthy parallel between the *Wunderkammer* and Fabergé's work is to be found not in each object by itself but in the appreciation and interpretation of the entire body of work. A *Wunderkammer* was admired not only for its marvelous objects in their own right but for its entirety as a cultural if not a social achievement: the possession and collection of a *cabinet de curiosité* was almost an essential part of the sixteenth-century prince's role. Similarly, the work of Fabergé, acquired by the royalty of his era, had for the collector an aura of distinguished taste. This aura has carried over today, tinged with a certain sense of nostalgia for a lost time, Fabergé being considered the epitome of an elegant society and lifestyle that has vanished.

A catalogue of the FORBES Magazine Collection, one of the few private collections on public view, was published in 1978. Since then the collection has been augmented, the most important acquisitions in 1979 being two Imperial Easter Eggs, the Coronation Egg and the Lilies of the Valley Egg. An updated catalogue of the collection appears in this book.

Miniature Coin Tankard, by Kollin, made of gold and set with gold rubles and sapphires.

It is the historical aspect and the imperial provenance of the pieces in this collection which distinguish it. Representing the oeuvre of Fabergé in a most comprehensive way, the collection has objects typical of all the different styles and techniques employed by the firm.

THE LONDON BRANCH

Fabergé's shop in London was only a branch of the main firm in St. Petersburg, which far overshadowed it in the number and importance of objects sold. But today the London branch has assumed greater importance for the studies of Fabergé's works, since the original documents of this shop have been discovered in the hands of the Fabergé family. These consist mainly of the sales ledgers—two leatherbound folio volumes—which give valuable information about the clientele, objects, and prices.

At the 1900 *Exposition Universelle* in Paris, where he displayed

Pair of Angel Fish, by Afanassiev, made of striated agate, rubies, nephrite, and green and red gold.

Opposite: Automated Rhinoceros, made of silver with a gold key. This is a mate to the rhinoceros given to Queen Alexandra as a sixty-fifth birthday present, now in a private collection.

several Imperial Easter Eggs, Fabergé received international recognition. Although he had many customers in Paris, it was to England that he came in 1903. This was because—until 1906—Fabergé was associated with three English brothers, Allan, Arthur, and Charles Bowe, and also because the potential clientele in England was as refined as it was wealthy, the ideal characteristics for Fabergé customers. Clearly, here was a combination of circumstances which must have been of commercial interest, suggesting the possibilities of successful representation in London. It should be remembered that while Fabergé employed almost 500 artists and craftsmen in his workshop, he only supervised the production—his métier was as an administrator and businessman.

The history of the English branch begins in 1903 with the dispatching of Arthur Bowe from Moscow to London bearing a selection of the firm's wares. Bowe set up an office in the Berners Hotel and began the first transactions. The Fabergé objects found immediate

Letter from Henry C. Bainbridge of the London branch of Fabergé.

acceptance. Many Englishmen who at that time were establishing industries in Russia already knew Fabergé's shop in St. Petersburg. Queen Alexandra had learned of the Fabergé objects from her sister, the Dowager Empress Marie Feodorovna. The Duchess of Marlborough, née Consuelo Vanderbilt, returned from a visit to Russia in 1902 laden with treasures from Fabergé, including the pink enameled egg-shaped serpent clock of imperial size and quality now in the FORBES Magazine Collection. In 1904 a charity bazaar exhibition of Fabergé, organized by Lady Arthur Paget, took place at the Royal Albert Hall.

After moving from the Berners Hotel, the branch office was briefly situated in Portland House, Duke Street, Grosvenor Square; but in 1906 it moved to 48 Dover Street. It remained there until 1911 when it was moved once again, this time to 173 New Bond Street. The first entry contained in the sales ledgers is for October 29, 1906, which, however, was later deleted. It would have confirmed the purchase of twenty-two objects by Queen Alexandra. Until the beginning of the detailed notes in October 1907, no further entries are recorded, despite the fact that the famous order of the Queen for the Sandringham menagerie in miniature must have taken place during this time. The reason for this one-year gap in the records must have been the reorganization of the London branch. Arthur Bowe left the firm; with the assistance of Henry C. Bainbridge, Nicholas Fabergé, Carl's youngest son, took over the direction of the London office.

From October 6, 1907, to January 9, 1917, all the sales were entered in the ledgers with the date, purchaser's name, description of the object, inventory number, sale price in pounds sterling, and cost of manufacture in rubles—an invaluable record! From 1908 on the details were entered in Bainbridge's handwriting.

The first entry was on October 6, 1907. The monthly account was recorded from the thirteenth of the month to the twelfth of the following month, and the sales were initially written up as the "new London branch total."

The best times of the year for selling the objects were at Easter and Christmas. These were also the seasons when a selection of items was taken to France: in December to Paris, in the spring to Nice, Cannes, and Monte Carlo. It was most probably Nicholas Fabergé or Henry Bainbridge who delivered the merchandise, solicited additional orders, and diligently acquired new clients.

The final ledger entry is for January 9, 1917. This is a surprising circumstance, insofar as it had always been assumed that the London branch closed down in 1915 in response to an imperial order that all capital abroad should be returned to Russia in order to finance the war. It is now clear that although the shop in New Bond Street was indeed closed, the business was nevertheless carried on for another two years by Bainbridge privately and without any restrictions.

In 1917 the remaining stock in London was bought by the French

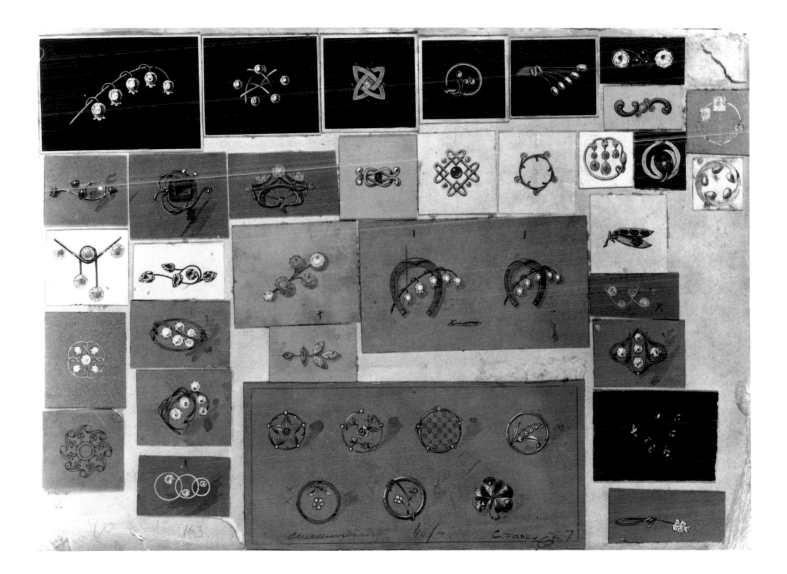

Left: Fabergé invoice from the Moscow branch bearing the "Great State Arms" with the imperial eagle.

Below: A page from an album of jewelry designs, probably by Oswald Jones, for Fabergé's Moscow branch.

Belt Buckle with Quiver, made of gold, white enamel, and rubies; Grand Duke Kirill Vladimirovich Cuff Links, made of white enamel, diamonds, and rubies for the son of Alexander III's brother; "Snowflake" Pendant with Red Cross, made of platinum, diamonds, rubies, rock crystal, and gold.

firm Lacloche Frères, of the Rue de la Paix, who marked the boxes of almost two hundred objects with their own trademark and sold them later. Lacloche had been cultivating business contacts with Russia, selling his own objects there and importing Russian objects into France since the turn of the century.

Hundreds of names are listed in the section of the London ledgers headed "Customer's Name." The clientele represented a Who's Who of fashionable and wealthy Edwardian society. Topping the list of notables were King Edward VII and Queen Alexandra. Although their visits to the shop were not frequent, usually a large number of objects were listed as their purchases. Many of the objects entered in the ledgers can still be found in the Royal Collections today. The "Frame, nephrite, ½ pearls, view in enamel of Sandringham; Nr. 17829, £67 (cost price 348 rubles)" we now know was bought by the Queen on November 28, 1908.

All those who were within the circle of the King's friends, and therefore represented Edwardian society by its very definition, are mentioned as clients who regularly visited the shop. Among these were the King's close friend, the Hon. Mrs. George Keppel, the financier Sir Ernest Cassel, Earl Howe, Lady Arthur Paget, the Duchess of Roxburghe, Lady Cooper, and the Hon. Mrs. Ronald Greville. On November 28, 1910, the last-named lady purchased "Dog 'Caesar', white onyx, brown enamelled collar with inscription 'I belong to the King', Nr. 18521, £35 (cost price 157 rubles)." Caesar was the King's favorite dog, who went everywhere with him and at Edward's funeral was carried behind the coffin even ahead of all his family and the foreign monarchs.

In 1909, on her sixty-fifth birthday, Queen Alexandra received an amusing present from the Lord Chamberlain, Earl Howe. This was—as recorded in the sales ledgers—a "Rhinoceros, Silver, mechanical movements, Nr. 17665 bought by Earl Howe on November 5, 1909

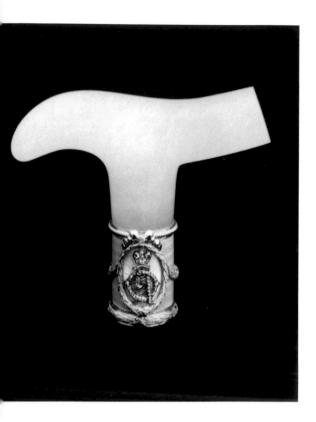

Imperial Parasol Handle, made of bowenite, gold, pink and white enamel, and diamonds, with the crowned monogram of Czarina Alexandra Feodorovna.

Opposite left: Miniature Watering Can, made of nephrite, diamonds, gold, and strawberry red enamel. It once belonged to Mme. Elizabeth Balletta, prima ballerina of the Imperial Michael Theater.

Opposite right: Miniature Basket of Lilies of the Valley, by Perchin, made of gold, pearls, and nephrite. It was once in the collection of Princess Marina, Dowager Duchess of Kent, the grandniece of Czar Alexander III.

for £60 (cost price 300 rubles)." Presumably Fabergé made two of these mechanical toys, as we find a similar one with the stock number 17591 in the FORBES Magazine Collection.

Leopold de Rothschild was another of the more famous clients at the London Fabergé's. He visited the shop regularly and placed large orders, procuring among other objects the Coronation Vase, described in the ledgers on April 12, 1911: "cup, rock crystal, engraved gold 72° enamelled, different stones, Nr. 18011, nett £430 (cost price 2,705 rubles)."

He presented this vase to King George V and Queen Mary at their coronation, having filled it with orchids from his garden in Gunnersbury. On December 7, 1911, he bought a "bonbonnière, blue and yellow striped enamel." These were the Rothschild racing colors, which became rather popular, judging by the number of objects that were ordered in these colors by other clients as well.

Additional names that appear time and time again are Mr. Stanislas Poklewski-Koziell, Councelor at the Russian Embassy, Princess Hatzfeld (née Claire Huntingdon from Detroit), Grand Duke Michael Michaelovich and his wife, the Countess Torby.

While in Paris, the Prince de la Moskowa and the Baronne Edouard de Rothschild were among the clientele; in London Fabergé had among his customers Lady Sackville, the Maharajah of Bikanir, Viscountess Curzon, Princess Cécile Murat, Empress Eugénie, the queens of Italy and Spain, King Manuel of Portugal, the Dowager Empress of Russia, and the Prince Aga Khan. The latter, for example, bought a "scent bottle, nephrite, gold mounts, red and white enamel" for £30 on October 18, 1913.

In only a few cases were cash sales made, and then the purchaser was listed in the ledgers as *Mr. X* or *Inconnu,* whether for reasons of privacy or snobbery we will never know. More often, however, presents to customers are openly recorded, as for example: "Gifts given in recognition of general services rendered," or "W. Koch's valet: tie pin, gratis."

The descriptions of the objects are short but precise. The materials used are given as well as the colors of the enamel. Apart from the especially famous clocks, boxes, frames, and miniature Easter eggs there are also more unusual objects mentioned which show the extraordinary versatility of Fabergé's craftsmanship. There are utilitarian items, for example: "clinical thermometers, menthol or tablet holders, crochet hooks," as well as figures of animals: "comic birds, pig (smiling), Borzoi, Zoubr, chameleon, Dachshund, Schattenvogel, elk, anteater, or gnus."

About 1908-9, objects that included pictures of houses and residences became fashionable. These views were painted in monochrome sepia on a pale pink opalescent ground which the Edwardians called "oyster" because of the mother-of-pearl effect.

A "Bonbonnière: Windsor and Balmoral, Nr. 15574" is the first

such residential scene in the sales ledger, sold to Sir Ernst Cassel on November 4, 1907, for £18/5. Apart from the Sandringham frame already mentioned on November 3, 1908, Queen Alexandra also bought a "Bonbonnière, nephrite, painted enamel view of Sandringham Alley, ½ pearls, Nr. 17651 £52/10," and on January 14, 1909, a "frame, painted in enamel of Windsor Castle, nephrite, gold and enamel border, Nr. 17883, £38." On the same day she purchased a "Bonbonnière, gold, pink painted enamel, 2 views of Chatsworth, & different enamels, Nr. 15662, £96," apparently as a present for the Duchess of Devonshire. According to Bainbridge, a similar box with a view of Knole, her home, was ordered by Lady Sackville.

The Grand Duke Michael Alexandrovich is on record as buying a cigar box with a view of the Houses of Parliament (November 6, 1908, Nr. 17313, £160); Earl Howe acquired a frame with a view of the Sandringham Church (November 24, 1908, Nr. 17769, £35); and Emanuel Nobel, a "Frame, jadeite, enamel, painted view Durham Abbey on gold 72° (Nr. 17995, £70)" on April 16, 1909.

An example of this painted oyster enamel, obviously made for the Russian clientele, is the box with a view of the Fortress of St. Peter

Overleaf: Top left: Rocaille Box, by Perchin, made of gold, royal blue and white enamel, and diamonds. The surprise miniature of Czar Nicholas II is concealed under his monogram.
Top right: Coronation Box, by Holmström, made of gold, gold and black enamel, and diamonds. Presented to Czar Nicholas II by his Czarina, Easter 1897.
Lower right: Castenskiold Imperial Presentation Case, by Holmström, made of gold, royal blue enamel, diamonds, and paste brilliants. Presented by Czar Nicholas II to Ludwig Castenskiold, equerry of the Czar's great uncle, King Christian IX of Denmark.
Bottom: Gold Imperial Presentation Cigarette Case, by Niukkanen.
Center left: Tortoiseshell Cigarette Case, with platinum, gold, and diamonds. Decorated in Art Nouveau style with flowering mustard-seed motifs.
Center: Nicholas II Nephrite Box, by Wigström, made of nephrite, diamonds, and green gold. Miniaturist, Zuiev.

and St. Paul in St. Petersburg. Another, made for the King of Siam, is illustrated on page 142.

A few statistics should give an idea of the production of the firm: between July 14, 1912, and July 13, 1913, Fabergé's customary fiscal year, 713 objects were sold. Most surprising is the large number of cigarette cases—a total of 91. Other favorites were 71 miniature Easter eggs, 25 animal figures, 23 picture frames; but only 8 table clocks were sold during this year.

The rarest of the objects are the flower studies and the hardstone figures. During the period between 1907 and 1917 when sales ledgers were being kept, almost 10,000 objects were sold, among which only 35 flower studies are mentioned. These included a vase of violets, a marguerite, or daisy, a raspberry bush, a jasmine, and a cactus. The most unusual and expensive flower, bought in 1908 for £117, is an enameled gold chrysanthemum spray with nephrite leaves standing in a square rock-crystal vase. It is now in the Royal Collection.

Surprisingly, Japanese flowers were very popular in 1907-8 in London, while none of the famous lily of the valley sprays, which nowadays are considered so typical of Fabergé's work, were sold.

Even more rare than the flower studies are the hardstone figures. There are only four mentioned in the sales ledgers:

> "John Bull," nephrite coat, white onyx waistcoat, yellow or-letz trousers, black obsidian hat, boots, gold stick, buttons, and watch chain. Nr. 17099 S. Polewski. £70.
>
> "Uncle Sam," white onyx hat, shirt and trousers, obsidian coat, orletz face, grey and red enamel waistcoat, gold watchchain and buttons. Nr. 17714 Mrs. W.K. Vanderbilt. £60.
>
> Model of a Chelsea Pensioner in pourpourine, black onyx, silver, gold, enamel, 2 sapphires. N. 18913 H.M. The King. £49.15s.
>
> Sailor, white onyx, orletz, lapis lazuli, black onyx, etc. Nr. 17634 Mme. Brassow. £53.

After the description of the object, there follows, as a matter of course, the inventory number. Every piece carries such a number. In most cases it is found on the metal base, scratched near the signature. Hardstone objects, especially the animal figures, which are usually unsigned, have a number in the sales ledger but do not have a number marked on them. The same applies to the miniature Easter eggs or the smaller pieces of jewelry, on which, because of their size, the stamp would scarcely be visible. Occasionally the inventory numbers can be found on the cloth-lined wooden cases, either scratched or written in ink.

With respect to marks and stamps on Fabergé objects sold in London, the English import marks should be mentioned. It is known that Fabergé refused to allow his objects to be controlled in England for technical reasons. This resulted in a court case against the Goldsmith's Company which Fabergé lost. The judgment of November 21, 1910, in the High Court of Justice basically referred to "enamelled objects" which henceforth had to be marked in London before completion. Plain silver or gold objects generally had to be marked when imported. Whereas the court was mainly concerned with the legal definitions of "plate" and "jewels and other stones" as used in the Customs Act (1842) and the Plate Act (1738) in connection with the enameling process for which the silver or gold was used, the Statement of Claim is of interest from today's point of view for the description of the activities of the House of Fabergé. Following is an excerpt from the High Court of Justice, Chancery Division, July 23, 1909 (F Nr. 651, Fos. 20):

> 1. The Plaintiff (Peter Charles Fabergé) is and for many years past has been carrying on at St. Petersburg in the Empire of Russia the business of designing and manufacturing articles of jewellery fantasy or vertu and other like articles of a very special kind being for the most part articles inlaid with enamel or set with precious stones on a foundation of gold or silver. In some of such articles both enamel and precious stones are used on a foundation of gold or silver.
>
> 2. The Plaintiff has and for some years past has had branch offices for the sale of the said articles in Moscow and elsewhere in the Empire of Russia and in London. All articles designed and manufactured by the Plaintiff as aforesaid are fully and finally completed at St. Petersburg before being consigned to such branch offices for sale.

Fabergé's luxury objects were always relatively expensive. The 713 objects listed in the year 1912-13, when the exchange was about $4.86 to £1, sold for £16,401, or for an average price of $112.

Generally the pieces were priced as follows: Miniature Easter eggs in simple enamel cost from 10s to £1, gold-mounted Easter eggs from £3 to £10; cigarette cases in silver £7 to £20, those with enamel £21 to £40, cigarette cases in hardstone—especially nephrite—£35 to £80, and in gold £63 to £120. Silver or gold-mounted wooden frames cost £4 to £7, and enamel frames £20 to £30. Table clocks ranged from £27 to £70 depending on the work involved, and the average price for the animal figures in hardstone was £25.

The flower studies cost between £20 and £117 and the rare hardstone figures between £49 and £70.

The most expensive objects were the pieces of jewelry, which were not in the usual Fabergé repertoire. A diamond tiara was sold to Mrs. Wrohan on December 14, 1909, for £1,400.

Today, it is very difficult for us to calculate the actual value of the prices mentioned. Our inflationary times offer little similarity in cost of living, and the 1912 pound, dollar, and ruble must be considered in relation to what they can buy now. As a comparison, according to the 1911 London *Baedeker,* a room at Claridge's Hotel as well as an à la

In the High Court of Justice.
CHANCERY DIVISION.

ROYAL COURTS OF JUSTICE,
Monday, 7th November, 1910.

BEFORE
MR. JUSTICE PARKER.

FABERGE—v.—THE GOLDSMITHS' COMPANY.

[Transcript of the Shorthand Notes of Messrs. H. H. TOLCHER & Co., 93 & 94, Chancery Lane, W.C., and Messrs. BARNETT & BARRETT, 40, Chancery Lane, W.C.]

Counsel for the Plaintiff: Sir ALFRED CRIPPS, K.C., M.P. Mr. MARK ROMER, K.C. and Mr. DIGHTON POLLOCK (instructed by Messrs. RAWLE, JOHNSTONE & Co., Agents for Mr. F. A. WOODCOCK, Manchester).

Counsel for the Defendants: Mr. S. O. BUCKMASTER, K.C., Mr. JOHN HENDERSON and Mr. R. F. GRAHAM-CAMPBELL (instructed by Messrs. PRIDEAUX & SONS).

SPEECH—FIRST DAY.

Sir ALFRED CRIPPS: My Lord, I appear for the Plaintiff in this case with my friends Mr. Mark Romer and Mr. Dighton Pollock; my friends Mr. Buckmaster, Mr. John Henderson and Mr. Graham-Campbell appear for the Defendants.

The point raised in this case is, as far as I know, a novel one, and certainly an important one, particularly to my client. The question is whether enamels and enamel work fall within the provisions for hall-marking by the Goldsmiths' Company under the head of either gold or silver plate, or gold or silver ware, or gold or silver manufacture. I am afraid I shall have to call your Lordship's attention at some length to the various sections of the Acts of Parliament. Some of them are rather complicated and I shall have to go through them in detail, but I will state first of all generally what the nature of the case is, and then I will call your Lordship's attention to the Sections of the Acts.

Your Lordship knows that enamelling is a very old art. We find it in Byzantine times, and of course we find very celebrated enamelling in the Middle Ages. Some of the most celebrated modern enamel is that which is manufactured in Russia by Mr. Faberge, who is the Plaintiff here. I will hand up to your Lordship specimens of the articles which it is alleged we ought to get hall marked before they are capable of being sold in this country.

Part of the document concerning Fabergé's court case against the Goldsmith's Company in London.

Opposite: "Big Bad Wolf" Lighter, by Rappoport, made of silver and red-glazed earthenware; Frog Ash Tray, made of bowenite, gold and garnets; Pig Match Holder/Striker, by First Silver *Artel,* made of silver and sandstone; Owl Bell Push, by Perchin, made of nephrite, tiger's-eye, two-color gold.

Ostrich Feather Fan by Wigström, made of gold, salmon-pink enamel, rock crystal, diamonds, mirror, ostrich feathers, and silk tassels. Carried by Grand Duchess Xenia, sister of Czar Nicholas II, at the seventeenth-century costume ball at the Winter Palace in February 1903.

carte dinner at the Ritz cost upwards of 10s 6d. A dozen oysters could be ordered for between 2s and 4s 6d. As far as the London Underground fares were concerned, the *Baedeker* said: "The fares are low: 1d-4d."

The last column in the ledgers has the manufacturing cost in rubles, showing that the markup was calculated at 90 to 100 percent. A number of objects were returned by customers, sometimes by persons other than the purchaser—most probably by recipients of a Fabergé gift exercising the time-honored prerogative of exchanging it. As an example, the "Japanese flower in bamboo" bought by Leopold de Rothschild for £35 on December 18, 1908, was later returned by the Countess of Carnarvon.

Pink Whistle, made of silver, silver gilt, and pink enamel; Festooned Fan by Wigström, made of gold, salmon-pink enamel, diamonds, and silk gauze; Pink Egg Cuff Links, by Wigström, made of gold and pink enamel; Oval Belt Buckle, by Perchin, made of silver gilt, pink enamel, and diamonds; Lorgnette with Octagonal Lenses, made of red gold, green gold, pink enamel.

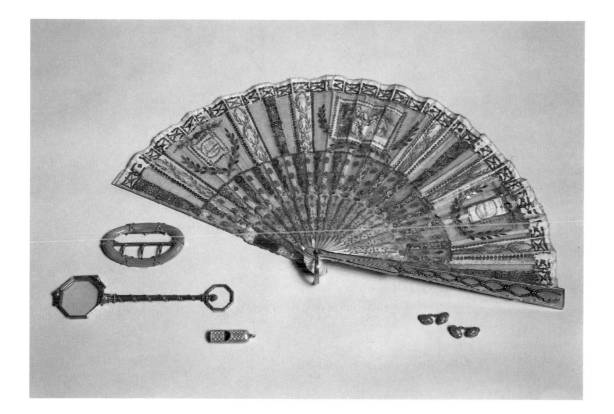

It was about the year 1884 that the firm of Fabergé, established in St. Petersburg in 1842, first began to produce *objets d'art et de fantaisie*. This innovation took place under the direction of Carl Fabergé, who had taken over the firm from his father, Gustav, in 1870, and who was joined in 1882 by his brother Agathon, a brilliant designer and artist.

The jeweler's and goldsmith's art had until then been characterized by a sumptuousness that took its cue from the flourishes of the baroque style. The industrial transformations in the mid-nineteenth century had led to a general level of prosperity, dramatized by high

PATRONS AND COLLECTORS BEFORE 1917

Grand Duchess Xenia seated at her desk in the summer residence, Mikhailovskoe, about 1915. A number of photograph frames, some by Fabergé, are displayed.

peaks of accumulated wealth and newly important fortunes. Under the influence of this recently monied class, the applied arts became ostentatious both in form and materials. A luxurious display of heavy diamond jewelry, massive gold bracelets, and diamond-encrusted objects was very much in vogue from 1840 to the 1880s.

From about the middle of the 1880s, the outright parading of wealth ceased in favor of a certain refinement and a more subtle relationship to ornamentation. Fabergé seemed to grasp the esthetic of this movement early on and completely changed the style of his hitherto traditional firm.

The astonishing success of his new productions was based on the fact that he now created jewelry and *objets de fantaisie* characterized by a refined and discreet elegance. He was more concerned with the visual impression created by a piece than with the value of the materials used; therefore his artists worked mainly with enamels, hardstones, and other decorative materials or techniques, instead of using brilliant diamonds and polished gold. This basic principle, combined with the apparently unlimited resources of his imagination, built the foundation of Fabergé's phenomenal success.

Another factor that had the positive effect of consolidating his success was the imperial patronage.

Patronage in art history generally means that a wealthy person or institution gives support to an artist not so much for his individual works as for the sake of art itself. Whereas the art lover might commission a specific work from the artist, the patron supports his work in general and leaves the artist complete freedom in the execution.

Fabergé was blessed with the opportunity of finding such a patron first in Czar Alexander III and later in his son Nicholas II. When in 1884 Alexander III asked Fabergé to make an Easter present for the Empress, the jeweler rose to the occasion brilliantly and the first of the series of Imperial Easter Eggs was created. It turned out to be such a success that the Czar placed a standing order for an egg every Easter. The one stipulation was that each egg must have a surprise enclosed in it. When Alexander III once asked what next year's surprise was to be, Fabergé is reported to have replied to the monarch only, "Your Majesty will be content."

The tradition of artistic patronage obligated the Czar to commission objects other than the Easter presents for his Empress. Alexander III obviously appreciated Fabergé's *objets d'art*, and imperial commissions for official presents were given increasingly to his firm.

As we know, Nicholas II followed his father in this custom and Eugène Fabergé, Carl's eldest son, reported that in the Winter Palace there was a special room where a wide selection of the firm's objects was kept. This stock of articles was available for official presents which were chosen by the chamberlain responsible for state gifts, or on rare occasions even by the Czar himself. Once a month Eugène Fabergé would spend time in that roomful of treasures to take stock, to prepare bills for the pieces that had been chosen, and to replenish the collection. Typical official presents were boxes decorated with the cipher or portrait of the Czar, cigarette cases, or frames with autographed photographs, all boxed in morocco cases with the Russian eagle applied on the cover.

The imperial patronage became official when the House of Fabergé received the appointment of "Goldsmith and Jeweler to the Imperial Court" in 1884. This appointment was customarily inscribed on a document headed by the imperial arms and stating the following: "The Chancellor of the Ministry of the Imperial Court herewith makes public that with the Highest approval—given on [date]—the jeweler [name] is granted the designation of Supplier of the Court of His Imperial Majesty with the right to show the representation of the Imperial Coat of Arms as above, with the inscription Supplier of the Court of his Imperial Majesty." Other jewelers, such as Cartier, who dealt with

Figure of John Bull, by Wigström, made of lapis lazuli, purpurine, and gold. Of the three known to exist, this one is from the collection of the late Sir Charles Clore, one is in the Thai Royal Collection, and another is mentioned in the London sales ledgers.

Opposite top: Dancing Moujik, made of yellow chalcedony, purpurine, black marble, pink agate, gray jasper, sapphires, and gold. Formerly in the Lansdell K. Christie Collection.

Opposite bottom: Captain of the 4th Harkovsky Lancers, by Wigström, made of lapis lazuli, tan and pink agate, obsidian, gold, silver, sapphires, and black and yellow enamel.

the Imperial Court had the right to display the "Small State Arms" with mantling and crown, but Fabergé was granted the "Great State Arms" showing the crowned imperial eagle. This was reproduced on all the invoices of the firm above the name "C. Fabergé" and "Joaillier de la Cour," as well as on the fitted wooden cases for his objects. The imperial warrant mark was used almost exclusively on pieces made in the Moscow workshops, although there were some exceptions.

For a society in which the Czar as absolute monarch represented the highest power, the imperial patronage and appointment as purveyor to the court had a stimulating effect on trade with the ruling circles. The Czar and the Imperial Family were trend setters, their taste sedulously aped by thousands of aristocrats, industrialists, and people of wealth who, following their monarch's example, started to buy and order from Fabergé. He was also the recipient of royal warrants from nearly all the European courts, and even from the king of faraway Siam. Between 1885 and 1917 it was fashionable to go to Fabergé's shops, and the resultant demand for his objects became so great that production had to be increased considerably. Fabergé finally employed up to 500 artists and workers, and a rough estimate of the quantity of objects produced by his workshops during the period from 1870 to 1917 may run as high as 100,000 pieces.

Photographs of the interiors of the Fabergé shops in St. Petersburg and Moscow show vitrines filled with objects in the distinctive pale wooden boxes. It is amusing—from the point of view of today's collectors—to imagine how customers could simply walk in and browse among the vitrines with the possibility of choosing from this immense stock of objects, simply buying whatever pleased them right over the counter.

The question arises, how did contemporaries of Fabergé look at these objects? Were they bought for collections? The answer to this question, which the author has repeatedly asked surviving émigrés, was nearly always negative. It seems only logical that purely utilitarian objects, such as table services, cutlery, claret jugs, all made mostly of silver, would not be considered collectors' items to be bought in large quantities. The same could apply to jewelry made exclusively of precious stones because their intrinsic value would limit the quantity. But these two categories—utilitarian objects and jewelry—were never considered typical Fabergé items.

Characteristically Fabergé are the *objets de fantaisie*, luxury objects of predominantly decorative value. But even these were usually not considered by Fabergé's contemporaries as items to be collected as art. There are several reasons for this rather dismissive attitude. First of all, one has to consider the interiors of nineteenth-century houses. It was common to have all sorts of bibelots scattered through the rooms, cluttering tabletops, desks, and commodes, or assembled on top of the ubiquitous piano. These were decorative trinkets of no practical use, very often souvenirs of an event or family occasion.

Here choices were influenced by nineteenth-century romanticism or the sentimental taste that prevailed. The strong sense of family, especially marked in the Imperial Family for dynastic reasons, created the vogue for portraits of family members to be displayed generously. Furthermore, since about 1880 photography had eclipsed silhouettes and hand-painted miniatures as portraiture, and consequently numerous portrait photographs in more or less valuable frames were displayed on every likely surface. This swarm of bibelots was part of the usual decor of the time, and even valuable objects, instead of being locked away in cabinets or vitrines, were scattered liberally throughout the rooms.

Another reason his contemporaries did not regard Fabergé's objects as serious works of art lies in Carl Fabergé's own notion of *objets de fantaisie*. His revolutionary idea was to introduce short-lived fashion into the production of precious jewelry.

Jewelry had been traditionally considered as a valuable investment to hold over a long period of time, even as precious heirlooms for future generations, so its designs were conservative. Fabergé changed all that, using the precious materials of a jeweler, but combining them in lighthearted designs for common objects of daily use such as bell-pushes, pillboxes, vanity cases, fans, étuis, and even clothing accessories such as belt buckles and cuff links. It is a matter of record that some women ordered their ballgowns to be made in colors matching the enamels of a favorite Fabergé piece.

Consequently, these items were bought primarily to be used or displayed for a relatively short period of time and were soon replaced by new ones responding to the current change of taste and fashion. This situates Fabergé in a modern context, abstracted from the nineteenth-century conception of the continuity of values.

Fabergé's production deferred to the changing fashions and he noted this in his catalogue (or Prix-Courant), published in Moscow in 1899, quoted here from a French translation by Eugène Fabergé in the collection of the late Léon Grinberg, Paris.

1. The products of our firm are frequently renewed due to the bizarre demands of fashion: new objects are offered for sale every day.
2. Some of our best objects cannot be published because we fear they will be imitated by our competitors.

The products of our firm are executed in our own workshops with materials of highest quality. The best artists, working exclusively for us, give us a variety of remarkably elegant designs which are as good as the best works of our foreign competitors. With regard to the Selection, we would like to mention the high quality of all sorts of articles in silver, gold, or brilliants in all kinds of designs including those of the latest fashion. With regard to the quality of our products, it will suffice to give our esteemed customers the four principles to which our production has rigorously submitted throughout the many years of our activity.

1. We only offer objects which are in perfect condition; this means, each item—even if the value is not higher than one Ruble—is fabricated with precision in all details.
2. We always try—and our customers can always rest assured of it—to offer a large quantity of newly designed articles. Old items which are out of fashion are not kept in stock: once a year they are collected and destroyed.
3. We always try to produce our articles in such a way that the value of an object corresponds to the sum of money spent on it; in other words, we are selling our objects as cheaply as the precise execution and workmanship permits.
4. Due to our considerable capital we are able to have a stock of a large quantity of articles both in variety and value which are offered to our esteemed customers.

This passage from the original Fabergé catalogue not only shows the acute consciousness of fashion, but also documents the salesmanship employed by the firm!

Fabergé's *objets de fantaisie* became increasingly popular, and in 1914 his firm was so famous that articles about his objects and the firm were published in the fashionable review *Stolitsa i Usadba* (*Town and Country*). In an interview dated January 15, 1914, Fabergé was asked, "Who buys these objects? This is all wasted money!" He answered, "There are people who already have enough of diamonds and pearls. Sometimes it is even not suitable to give jewelry as a present, but such a small object is the right thing."

Fabergé offers one of the main reasons why his contemporaries were buying his objects: they were fashionable presents. In his book on Fabergé, H. C. Bainbridge reported it similarly: "Except in rare cases, I never remember the Edwardian ladies buying anything for themselves; they received their Fabergé objects as gifts from men, and these gifts were purely for the psychological moment. When that had passed, i.e., the actual moment of the giving, they completed the mission for which they had been made."

Even if Fabergé objects were generally considered as bibelots, fashion accessories, or small presents, certain rare types of objects were made especially for customers who collected them as *objets d'art*. These were the large Easter eggs, composite hardstone figures, and flower arrangements. They represent Fabergé's creative genius at its best and were as rare and valuable during his lifetime as they are today.

The Easter eggs were originally made exclusively for the Imperial Family. Later, wealthy private customers such as Prince Youssoupoff, the mining magnate Alexander Kelch, and the oil tycoon and industrialist Emanuel Nobel also ordered elaborate eggs. Nobel, regarded by Fabergé as his most important nonaristocratic patron, also had a large collection of hardstone figures representing Russian folk types, of which about thirty were made by Fabergé. Some of them were por-

Rückert Cigarette Case, made of silver, moss-green, blue, and aubergine enamel, with sapphire push button; in the Pan-Slavic or Old Russian Style. Original case is stamped with Imperial Warrant.

trait models—for example, the figurines of the Cossack bodyguards of the Empresses, especially commissioned by Nicholas II.

Although they were produced in greater numbers than the hardstone figurines, the flower arrangements of gold, enamel, and hardstone in rock crystal vases were collected as *objets d'art*.

The few exhibitions of Fabergé objects organized before 1917 mainly featured the Imperial Easter Eggs, which always attracted great attention. The first public exhibition of Easter eggs was the *Exposition Universelle* of 1900 in Paris, where some of them were shown at the special request of the Empresses.

It is of great interest to learn from the *Rapports du Jury International* (*Joaillerie*), published in 1902, of the appreciation of Fabergé's work by his contemporaries:

> One has to express one's satisfaction when examining one by one and in detail the jewels exhibited *hors concours* by the House of Fabergé, who is a member of the Jury. This work reaches the ex-

This group of small picture frames, the largest of which is 4¼ inches, illustrates the inimitable technical perfection of the Fabergé style, "luxurious but discreet."

Opposite top: Circular Softwood Frame, by Nevalainen, made of wood, silver, and silver gilt. Once owned by Czarina Marie Feodorovna, it contains a photograph of Grand Duchess Xenia.

treme limits of perfection, it means the transformation of a jewel into a real *objet d'art*. It is the perfect execution, completed with precise setting, which distinguishes all the objects exhibited by Fabergé. This may be seen on the miniature imperial crown set with 4000 stones, or the enamel flowers which are so perfectly imitated that they could be regarded as natural plants—or all the many *articles de fantaisie* which have been examined by the Jury at length.

Another exhibition was held in 1902 in St. Petersburg as a charity event at the Palace of Grand Duke Vladimir Alexandrovich. The main attraction was the group of Imperial Easter Eggs and a variety of Fabergé items belonging to the Czar the Empresses, and other members of the Imperial Family, "as well as to Prince Youssoupoff, Count Sumarokov-Elston, Count Benckendorff—and other persons from highest circles," as reported in *Niva, The Illustrated Journal of Literature and Contemporary Life*, that March.

This brings us back to the original question: Who was buying or collecting Fabergé objects before 1917? Unfortunately, there are no records preserved from the main House of Fabergé in St. Petersburg like the sales ledgers of the London branch, which could give an idea of the clientele. As we have seen, the Imperial Family was by far the greatest client of Fabergé. All the Grand Dukes and Duchesses bought his objects. Grand Duchess Marie Pavlovna, who also patronized Cartier in Paris, and the Grand Duchess Elizabeth Feodorovna, sister of the Empress, often came personally to the shop in St. Petersburg, while other members of the Imperial Family received regular visits from Fabergé himself, or one of his sons, who would show them the new collections. The Empress Alexandra ordered hundreds of objects each Christmas as presents for her family, the Ladies-in-Waiting, and other members of the Court. She and the Dowager Empress Marie became—unwittingly—the best international publicity agents for Fabergé when they sent presents to their royal relations scattered all over Europe. In this way Queen Alexandra of England, sister of Empress Marie, first became acquainted with works by Fabergé. She was ultimately one of his most avid customers.

Many pieces were given as presents by Empress Alexandra to her sister, the Princess Henry of Prussia, and to her brother, the Grand Duke of Hesse-Darmstadt. Other royal courts, especially those of Denmark, Sweden, Greece, and Rumania, acquired objects directly at Fabergé's. Another patron was King Ferdinand of Bulgaria, who regularly commissioned large numbers of objects from Fabergé. He also decorated the jeweler with the Bulgarian Order of St. Alexander. Most exotic of all of Fabergé's royal customers was King Chulalongkorn of Siam—but the account of his collection appears in a later chapter of its own.

Apart from royalty, nearly all the Russian aristocrats as well as the wealthy industrialists came to buy at Fabergé's shop. Official

Heart Surprise Frame of enameled gold set with diamonds and pearls. Open, it displays miniature portraits of Czar Nicholas II, Czarina Alexandra, and Tatiana, their second daughter, whose birth in 1897 the frame commemorates.

presents from institutions, regiments, and firms were ordered from the House of Fabergé.

The circle of those who patronized, gave, and received objects by Fabergé seems to be completed with the coronation gift from the merchants of Nijni-Novgorod to the Empress Alexandra. This was the famous Lily of the Valley Basket which the Empress kept always on her desk and which now resides in the Matilda Geddings Gray Collection in New Orleans.

COLLECTORS, SALES, AND EXHIBITIONS: 1918-1945

A document relating to the purchase in 1934 of a Fabergé cigarette case by Queen Mary from Prince Vladimir Galitzine, who had emigrated to England. The case is still in the Royal Collection.

Following the outbreak of the 1917 October Revolution in Petrograd (formerly St. Petersburg), a "Committee of the Employees of the Company K. Fabergé" was formed. It took over the management of the firm until November 1918, when Fabergé emigrated with the aid of the British Embassy. With his departure, the firm ceased to exist. (The London branch had officially been closed down in 1915 although, as we now know, sales of objects had continued until January 1917.)

It was, in fact, the end of an epoch—signaled by the World War, the Russian Revolution, and the fall of kings and empires. The historical and social upheavals contributed to the changing attitude toward the *objets de luxe* created by Fabergé. There was an increasing taste for simplicity and geometric styles—art deco became all the vogue— and Fabergé's once-fashionable objects were no longer in style.

An example of this swing in taste away from Fabergé comes from the son of Monsieur Lacloche, who had acquired the remaining stock of about two hundred pieces from Fabergé's London branch. He reported that the firm had great difficulty disposing of these items in London and Paris, and did not manage to sell off the last of them until 1923.

By that time, thousands of Russian émigrés had arrived in the West. In order to survive they were forced to sell their jewelry, including those Fabergé objects which they had managed to bring out of Russia. The art market was suddenly inundated with objects no longer in fashion. Often they were bought only for the value of their precious metal, which was then melted down, or for the stones, which were remounted. In the history of Fabergé, this period is recorded as the most disastrous, since many unique items were destroyed, the priceless workmanship lost forever.

From the records of Léon Grinberg, of A La Vieille Russie in Paris, we know that in 1920 a number of Fabergé Easter eggs had already appeared on the market. They were offered for sale by the jeweler Morgan in the Rue de la Paix in Paris. Because of French hallmarking regulations they could not be exhibited, and Grinberg was at first hesitant to buy them. In this fabulous clutch of eggs were included the Hen Egg, the Pine Cone Egg, the Rocaille Egg, the Bonbonnière

Egg, the Apple Blossom Egg, and the Chanticleer Egg—all of which Grinberg finally bought en bloc for 40,000 francs ($3,000)!

It is interesting that only two years after the death of the Czar the question of the imperial provenance of these Easter eggs was raised. Grinberg writes in his diary: "Morgan himself did not know to whom these eggs originally had belonged. Judging from the exceptional richness, they must be imperial Easter presents. We think they were presented by the Grand Duke Alexei Alexandrovich to the ballet dancer Mrs. Balletta." This is corrected in a penciled note: "Alexander Fabergé [Carl's third son] told us that these eggs were made for a very rich industrialist as presents for his wife Barbara. Eggs of such richness were only made for K[elch] or the Court."

It took several years to sell the six Easter eggs—until 1928, when they were bought as a group by an American collector for the total sum of 200,000 francs ($7,800).

This figure is an indication of the depressed market and the limited interest in Fabergé objects during this period. For example, the Marlborough Egg was donated by the former Duchess of Marlborough, then Mrs. Jacques Balsan, to a charity bazaar in Paris where it was sold in 1927.

To illustrate the state of the Fabergé market at the time, it is interesting to reprint part of a newspaper article published in *The World* on August 2, 1925, under the title "Jewels From Hidden Vaults Stream Into America."

At the close of the year, the stream [of jewels] grew to huge proportions. In the first five months of 1919, importations of precious stones from London alone to America reached $75,000,000. American buyers went abroad to bid on jewels of defunct royalties. Hitherto unobtainable jewels were offered at public sales. The coffers of the old world were thrown open.

Foremost in the minds of prospective buyers, however, were the enormous treasures of Russia. The exact extent of these no one knew, not even the Russians themselves, as it afterwards proved. Besides the crown jewels proper, Russia had incalculable reserves of jewels in the caskets of its noble families. Collectors watched with eagerness and diamond merchants with some uneasiness, for the appearance of these treasures.

They soon appeared. Starving nobles sold pearls to buy bread, bribed with diamonds for escape and paid with emeralds for their lives. Jewels from all sorts of mysterious sources began to trickle by roundabout ways into the great gem markets of the world—and America is the greatest. They appeared in New York City, quietly and unexplained. They were caught now and then by the customs authorities; they probably found their way to many a pretty American finger whose owner never suspected their origin.

Doubtless many privately owned Russian jewels offered for sale abroad were incorrectly assumed to be Russian crown jewels. Reports were definite and persistent, however, that the Soviet Government was offering quantities of gems—whether

Overleaf: Desk pieces: clockwise from left, nephrite paper knife, round magnifying glass, square magnifying glass, fleur-de-lys bowenite bookmarker, rock crystal bookmarker, book blade, and loupe.

crown gems or not—to raise funds for its needs. It was said that it paid 2,000,000 rubles in diamonds to finance the war with Poland. Jewels and art treasures said to have belonged to the Romanoffs found their way to London auction rooms so regularly that they excited no curiosity and brought no more than normal prices. The Grand Duke Boris sold 4,000,000 francs worth of diamonds and emeralds in Paris, and it was reported that Prince Youssoupoff about the same time pawned to Hugo Stinnes in Berlin a quantity of what were said to be Romanoff family jewels for about 60 percent of their value.

While this article gives an idea of the scope of the jewelry market in the United States and Western Europe, the question remaining was, what had happened to the Russian art collections in the Soviet Union since the Revolution? A rare account of this is given in *Art Treasures in Soviet Russia* by Sir Martin Conway, who traveled there in the summer of 1924:

> The Bolshevik theory is that the great landowners of Russia had no right to the land, and therefore that all their possessions were likewise improperly acquired, and ought to be regarded as public property. [In Moscow] I was led into a room, where I saw 26,000 pieces of silver plate in the process of being studied and classified—countless teapots and coffee-pots and other objects of domestic utility of small artistic merit and no public interest. I noted long rows of pineapple-cups, mainly of late eighteenth-century German manufacture, quantities of tankards and beakers, candlesticks and soup-tureens, and every kind of utensil. The sight of such a number of second- and third-rate objects was wearying. One was forced to conclude that there are only two ways of profitably disposing of this mass of silver, either to send most of it to the melting-pot or to sell it off into private ownership once more.
>
> It goes without saying that much privately owned jewellery must have fallen into the hands of the State.

In 1927 the Soviets unofficially started to sell works of art in order to receive currencies. The first sale was held on March 16, 1927, at Christie's in London: "an important assemblage of Magnificent Jewellery mostly dating from the 18th Century, which formed part of the Russian State Jewels." Other sales followed, mainly in Berlin at Lepke, where "Works of Art from the Museums and Palaces of Leningrad" were sold in November 1928. But pieces by Fabergé—now out of fashion—were not included in these sales. Fabergé objects were for the most part bought directly in Moscow or Leningrad by entrepreneurs and art dealers such as Dr. Armand Hammer, Alexander Schaffer, and Emanuel Snowman, who started to form collections of Fabergé objects chiefly for later resale. Dr. Hammer had acquired fifteen Imperial Easter Eggs during the 1920s which he later placed on sale in the United States. In *Fabergé Eggs* he writes: "Wherever the sales took place, the Fabergé eggs were a great center of attraction, even though difficult to sell in the middle of the depression."

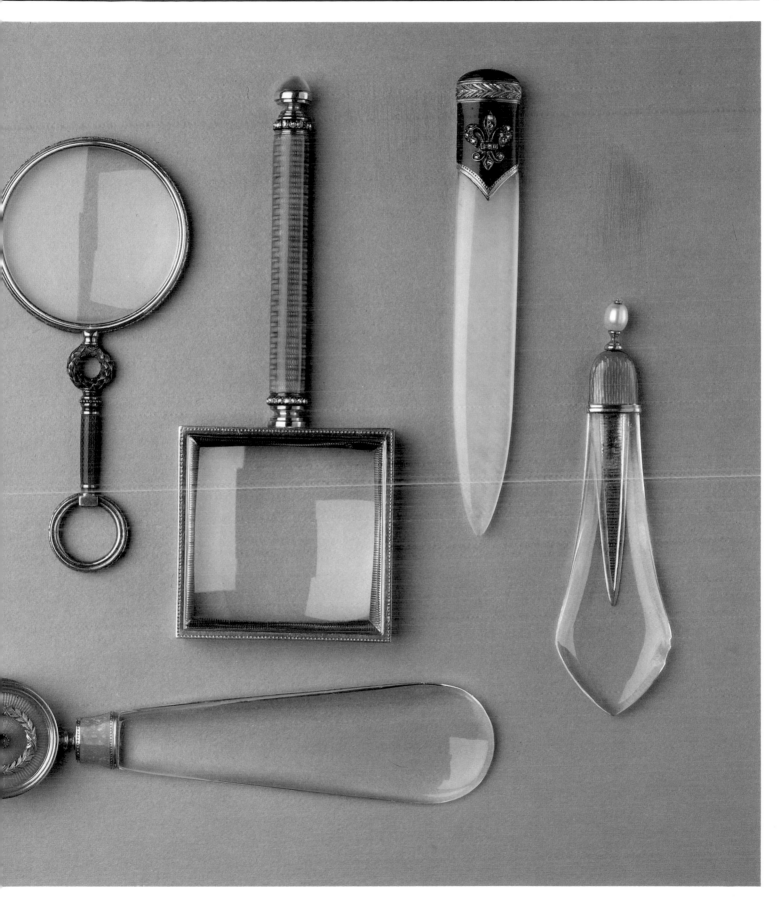

One of the keenest collectors in Europe during the 1920s was Queen Mary, wife of King George V of England, who continued to increase the Royal Collection of Fabergé initiated by King Edward VII and Queen Alexandra. Queen Mary was known in Russian émigré circles as an eager buyer of their treasures. She also patronized Wartski, the jewelers whose owner, Emanuel Snowman, had been among the first to purchase a number of objects from the Soviets. In the Wartski stockbooks of the 1920s, page after page of stone animal carvings by Fabergé are listed, costing then between £1 and £5 each. On November 26, 1927, Queen Mary bought a miniature nephrite grand piano for £75 ($363), and on October 12, 1929, she acquired the Colonnade Egg for £500 ($2,425), objects which are still in the Royal Collection.

The recovery of the market for Fabergé and the beginning of modern collecting of these treasures can be dated to the year 1933. In the United States it was a series of exhibitions of Russian art organized by Dr. Hammer that attracted great publicity and attention. His was the audaciously original idea of selling Fabergé and Russian art through American department stores. Later he and his brother Victor opened the Hammer Galleries in New York.

On January 2, 1933, the *New York Times* carried the following story:

> JEWELRY OF CZAR ON VIEW THIS WEEK. GIFT EASTER EGGS ENCRUSTED WITH GEMS AMONG PIECES BOUGHT IN RUSSIA BY DR. HAMMER.
>
> Memories of the splendor that surrounded the Russian royal family before its members were killed in July, 1918, are to be revived on Fifth Avenue tomorrow, when a $1,000,000 collection of jewels and objects of art from the Russian royal palaces will be placed on view at Lord & Taylor.
>
> Collected by Dr. Armand Hammer, who purchased the items out of his profits from concessions held under the Soviet Government, including one which for a time gave him a monopoly in Russia on lead pencils and stationery, the gems and other items of the collection are to be shown tomorrow at a preview, to which admission is by invitation only. On Wednesday the exhibit will be opened to the public, and will remain on display for three weeks. Chief among the jewels illustrating the generosity of the Czar are two Easter eggs. One, presented by the Czar to the Czarina on Easter morning 1912, is fashioned from lapis lazuli, heavily ornamented with gold. Inside the egg, which opens like a jewel case, is a replica of the Russian eagle fashioned from large diamonds. The second egg, of gold and enamel, set with diamonds and emeralds, was presented by Nicholas on Easter 1895, to the Queen Dowager Marie Feodorovna. It serves as a case for a gold screen with ten mother-of-pearl panels, on which are miniatures of the eight castles she occupied during her girlhood in Denmark, and of her two yachts.

The exhibitions organized by Dr. Hammer and others initiated the collecting of Fabergé in the United States. During the 1930s, collections of Fabergé objects including Imperial Easter Eggs were formed by Mrs. Marjorie Merriweather Post (they are now at Hillwood, her former home in Washington, D.C.), Mrs. Lillian Thomas Pratt (now in the Virginia Museum of Fine Art in Richmond), Mrs. Matilda Geddings Gray (now in the Gray Foundation, on loan to the New Orleans Museum), and by Mrs. India Early Minshall (now in the Cleveland Museum of Art).

Mrs. Gray began to collect Fabergé objects after seeing Dr. Hammer's precious hoard at the Chicago World's Fair in 1934. She eventually owned three Imperial Easter Eggs and the celebrated Lily of the Valley Basket of Empress Alexandra Feodorovna.

It was not only in America that the public became aware of Fabergé's creative genius, but also in Europe. Appreciation that had flagged began to increase by the mid-1930s. In 1934, a series of articles, "Russian Imperial Easter Gifts, the Work of Carl Fabergé," had been published by Fabergé's old London manager, H. C. Bainbridge, in *Connoisseur*. The introduction to the first of these articles stated: "Much interest was aroused recently by the appearance at a public sale, of the first of a series of Easter eggs made by Carl Fabergé for the

Imperial Presentation Tray by Wigström, made of nephrite, two-color gold, strawberry-red enamel, and diamonds. The handles are mounted with the crowned monograms of Czar Nicholas II and Czarina Alexandra Feodorovna.

late Imperial Russian Family." That sale was held at Christie's on March 15, 1934, and included 87 Fabergé objects crowned with two Imperial Easter Eggs, the First Imperial Egg and the Resurrection Egg, which fetched £85 ($425) and £110 ($550) respectively.

In 1935 the London Exhibition of Russian Art in Belgrave Square attracted great attention. Unlike the American Fabergé exhibits, which displayed items recently acquired from the Soviet government, the London exhibit was primarily formed of items belonging to the English Royal Family and to collections assembled prior to 1917, including those of Mademoiselle Yznaga del Valle, Lady Zia Wernher, and Lady Juliet Duff. The exhibition, comprising more than 150 Fabergé pieces, included five Imperial Easter Eggs.

During the late 1930s and 1940s several important collections of Fabergé objects were formed, including those of Sir Bernhard Eckstein, Mr. Gordon-Bois, and King Farouk of Egypt. Sir William Seeds, who had been the British ambassador to Moscow, bought the celebrated collection of eleven composite hardstone figures in 1941.

CONTEMPORARY COLLECTING

Tumble Cup, made of silver gilt with black, olive green, royal blue, light blue, white, yellow, pink, and beige enamel. Designed in the Pan-Slavic style, this piece retains its original paper Fabergé label.

With the end of the Second World War a new era of collecting began. The Soviets stopped selling art, so collectors of Fabergé were now limited exclusively to those pieces already located in the West. Considering that a great number of items were already held in private collections, trusts, or foundations, mainly in the United States, the existing Fabergé market became increasingly sparse.

Each important collection that came on the market was eagerly snapped up by the steadily growing number of new collectors. Milestones were reached, such as the Eckstein sale in 1947 which included the Winter Egg, the King Farouk Collection in 1954 which included sixty-five lots of about 150 Fabergé objects, and in 1959, the collection of Sir Charles Dodd. One of Europe's most discerning collectors at the time was the Swiss Maurice Sandoz, who owned some of Fabergé's finest works such as the Orange Tree Egg, the Peacock Egg, the Swan Egg, and the Youssoupoff Egg. This collection was partially dispersed just before and after the death of the owner.

In the 1960s, Fabergé prices took a leap. Single items or smaller properties were sold, sometimes by the original buyers or their descendants, as for example the Cross of St. George Egg that came up for auction in 1961. When it was sold at Sotheby's by Prince Vassily Romanov—the son of Grand Duchess Xenia, who had inherited it from her mother, the Dowager Empress Marie Feodorovna—it fetched £11,000 ($30,000).

Another collector of Fabergé objects was the shipping magnate Lansdell Christie of Long Island. His collection included, among others, the Chanticleer Egg, the Spring Flower Egg, and the Kelch Hen

Egg, which were exhibited for a time at The Metropolitan Museum of New York. In 1966 this fine collection was up for sale.

Malcolm S. Forbes had started to collect objects by Fabergé around 1960 for the FORBES Magazine Collection, and he seized the opportunity to buy the most important items from the Christie collection. To this nucleus he has constantly added more objects, thus forming a treasure trove of more than 200 pieces, now one of the finest Fabergé collections in the world. On a much smaller scale, but known for the pair of elegant opera glasses and fine pieces carved in nephrite, is the collection of the late Bing Crosby, now owned by his widow.

Other collections which made their name in the Fabergé world were those of Robert Strauss and Josiane Woolf, sold by Christie's in 1976 and 1980-81 respectively. While at the Strauss sale great interest was shown in the Fabergé flower arrangements, the Woolf sale is memorable for the high prices its hardstone figures commanded, including a whopping SF 410,000 ($235,000) for the figure of a Russian peasant seated on a bench and playing the balalaika, which previously had belonged to Sir William Seeds.

The growing interest in Fabergé was recently demonstrated by the enthusiasm with which crowds came to view the Exhibition of Fabergé at the Victoria and Albert Museum in 1977. The majority of the items shown belonged to the Queen of England, who owns one of the largest private collections of Fabergé objects in the world. Part of this collection was again exhibited in 1983 at the Cooper Hewitt Museum in New York, where it attracted great public attention. It is rare for Fabergé objects to be on public display, a circumstance which greatly enhances their fascination.

Cipher of Czarina Alexandra Feodorovna under finial table diamond with chased gold palmette surround. Detail on top of Fifteenth Anniversary Egg.

Generally it can be said that the collecting of Fabergé is predominantly within the private domain. Public museums are rarely interested in buying. Due to strict tax laws, as well as security and insurance problems, the acquisition of Fabergé objects is undertaken with great discretion if not with secrecy. Although a number of objects are sold at public auctions each year, it is difficult to ascertain the identity of the actual buyers, as they are normally represented in the sale rooms by leading art dealers. As a result of this secrecy, there are rumors that the Queen is still acquiring pieces for her collection or that the Aga Khan buys Fabergé hardstone figures. There are only a few important contemporary collectors, such as Malcolm Forbes, who choose to make their collections accessible to the general public.

With the growing interest in Fabergé's works there are, of course, a number of anonymous collectors who have created substantial collections. Collectors of Fabergé objects tend to specialize in one of the following categories:

- *Objects of use:* Primarily silver or silver-mounted pieces like cutlery, plates, carafes, vases, and centerpieces.

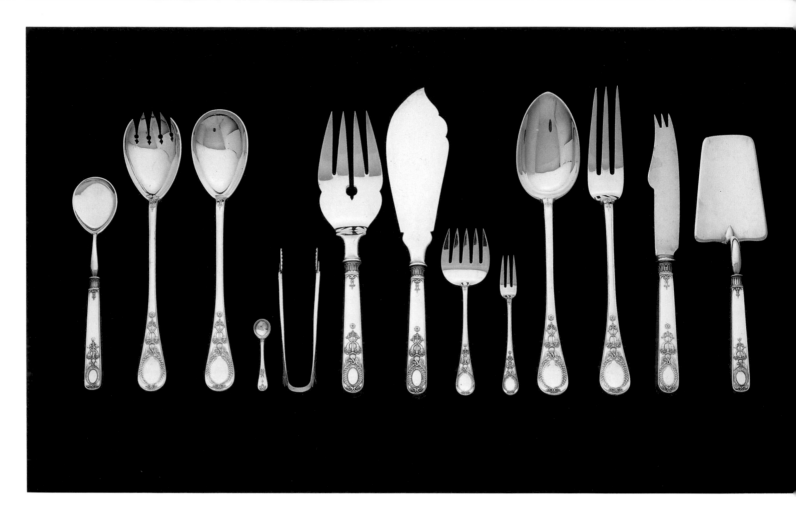

Empire-Style Silver and Silver Gilt Table Service, 370 pieces, made in the Moscow branch.

- *Enamels:* The different color schemes of enamels as well as the different guilloché patterns are points of interest for some discerning collectors. Still others admire the cloisonné enamels from the Moscow workshop of Fedor Rückert.
- *Hardstone objects:* The example of King Edward VII and Queen Alexandra, who had a whole menagerie of miniature animals made by Fabergé in hardstone, is still followed by contemporary collectors. More exclusive because of their rarity are collections of composite hardstone flower arrangements.

This list of collectible categories could be continued, for the simple reason that Fabergé had a most comprehensive and versatile output of objects. This variety, combined with a certain nostalgia for imperial splendor, makes the collecting of Fabergé pieces so attractive. However, it must be said that the most important collections are those which have one of each category of the objects created by Fabergé. Recently this inclusiveness has become more difficult, if not impossible, as Imperial Easter Eggs no longer seem to appear on the open art market.

The style of Fabergé objects was luxurious but discreet. This would explain the high prices attained for small bric-a-brac signed with the precious signature of a firm which was by appointment to imperial and royal courts. Fabergé's reputation was already so great by 1900 that a number of envious goldsmiths and jewelers started to copy him, although they never achieved the extraordinary quality of his objects. Among these contemporary imitators of Fabergé were artists and firms like Tillander, Bolin, Hahn, Sumin, and especially Britzin, as well as minor artists and firms.

During the 1920s, when a lack of interest in Fabergé items was most apparent, it is understandable that the problem of Fabergé imitations never really arose, although Cartier continued the Fabergé style in Paris, notably with hardstone flower ornaments. At that time Eugène Fabergé had started "Fabergé & Cie" in Paris, but with no great success.

It is of interest to note that at the beginning of the 1930s when Fabergé objects were once again being collected, Bainbridge apparently felt obliged to include in an article, published in *Connoisseur* in

COPIES AND FORGERIES

Louis XVI-Style Snuffbox, by Perchin, made of gold, green, red, and white enamel, and diamonds, with a painted enamel plaque representing Venus and Cupid. Made in response to Czar Alexander III's challenge that Fabergé could not improve upon the craftsmanship of eighteenth-century French goldsmiths such as Etienne Blerzy. A Louis XVI snuffbox is at left.

1934, "particulars which will assist collectors to confirm the genuineness of Fabergé pieces." He also wrote, "The much wider interest, since the house of Fabergé ceased to exist, made the identification a matter of importance."

About 1945, books on Fabergé's oeuvre began to be published. Their illustrations provided fraudulent jewelers with basic material for inspiration. Copies were made directly after the photographs, especially of hardstone objects such as animal figures.

The escalating prices for Fabergé objects during the 1960s and 1970s similarly encouraged the production of fake enamels, including copies of Imperial Easter Eggs, very often of appalling quality, which nevertheless found buyers.

Apart from counterfeiting marks and signatures, the forger's most difficult problem is imitating Fabergé's exceptional technical perfection.

Nowadays there is no guilloché enamel, chasing, and setting that can compete with Fabergé's, although to the uneducated eye they may come close. In fact, the only real aid in discerning the genuine object from a fake is the study and comparison of the smallest details, such as hinges, guilloché patterns, and the setting of stones, as well as the rather complicated system of marks and signatures.

Finally, it is amusing to read from B. Bucher's introduction to a book on forgeries written nearly a century ago (*Fälscherkunste* by P. Eudel). From today's point of view, it illustrates a classical problem in the art market:

> The business of faking has always flourished, since antiques were first collected, and it flourishes . . . nowadays especially, since collecting has become a general fashion. The demand is so significant that the supply of genuine articles has been insufficient; the prices have risen to a height that makes the faking of objects more profitable than doing original work. By cleverly repairing damages, by restituting a missing piece, by adding a signature, etc., the value of an object can be quadrupled, even multiplied by ten. But the art of so-called restoration presupposes an old piece. The enterprising forger does not stop here; by remolding, copying, imitating he finally becomes a "creating artist."

54

First Imperial Egg, 1885. The FORBES
Magazine Collection, New York.

Opposite: Resurrection Egg, possibly 1889,
by Perchin. The FORBES Magazine
Collection, New York.

IMPERIAL EASTER EGGS

The Imperial Easter Eggs have always been considered Fabergé's chefs d'oeuvre. In every respect they represent the epitome of his work: in style, technical quality, and importance of materials used, they were the best he produced.

The historical background of the Easter egg is well known. Since early Christian times it was a symbol of the Resurrection of Christ, and later a symbol of life itself. Easter, the most important of the Orthodox Church feasts, has given rise to the deepest feelings and the most joyous celebrations in Russia, where the Easter season coincides with the beginning of spring, a release from the long ice-bound winter. "Christ is risen!" is the jubilant greeting on this happiest of holidays.

The smooth shape of an egg, with the harmonious proportions of its form, is very pleasing to the eye and to the touch. Not surprisingly, it has always attracted artists and especially goldsmiths and jewelers, who favored egg-shaped *objets d'art*. During the eighteenth century, egg-shaped *nécessaires* —chiefly gold-mounted hardstone étuis (small ornamental cases) and patch-boxes for the ladies' beauty marks—were produced in France, England, and Germany. An incense burner made in the shape of an egg by Jean-Jacques Duc for

Catherine the Great about 1770 was kept in the Treasury of the Hermitage, to which, a century later, Fabergé had access and which apparently served him as a source of inspiration. In the nineteenth century, egg-shaped objects continued to be very much in fashion. Enameled gold or silver-gilt eggs which opened to reveal a chicken that in turn served as a container for a jewel were made in Germany and in Vienna around 1850. Two of these eggs appeared recently at auction, one recorded in Christie's London sale catalogue, November 18, 1969, lot 150 (the case bearing the mark of Moritz Elimayer), the other in Christie's Geneva sale catalogue, May 10, 1983, lot 73 (Vienna, maker's mark J W).

At the end of the 1870s the St. Petersburg goldsmith Joseph Nordberg made a silver-gilt Easter egg supported by four Orthodox crosses and decorated with the blue enameled cipher of Czar Alexander II. This egg, which was kept in the Alexander Palace of Tsarskoe Selo, opens to reveal an icon of the Virgin Vladimirskaya.

All these examples of egg-shaped *objets d'art* indicate the extent to which Fabergé was heir to a tradition that combined the European goldsmith's art with a Russian Easter custom. Independent from the work of Fabergé, other egg-shaped objects were made by Russian artists until 1917. These include cloisonné enamel eggs, miniature egg pendants, and also porcelain and lacquer eggs.

The question arises: What makes Fabergé Easter eggs so special? He did not originate the idea of creating eggs out of precious materials as *objets d'art* or jewels. It was, however, Fabergé's genius to take an existing tradition and develop it to the highest quality. This excellence includes both the materials used and the incredible workmanship lavished on each piece as well as the astonishing versatility exhibited in the decoration of the eggs. The concept of creating a series of superlative Easter eggs for the Imperial Family over a period of more than thirty years is without parallel in the history of the applied arts. This feat earned Fabergé his place in history as one of the last great jeweler-artists in a tradition of imperial patronage and court art that was to disappear with the Revolution.

Books and studies on Fabergé have always attempted to date the Imperial Easter Eggs and to list them in chronological order. Of the surviving eggs made by Fabergé, twenty-eight carry a date, either next to the signature in the enamel decoration or under table-cut diamonds. While the majority of the eggs made during the period from 1900 to 1917 are dated in this fashion, those of the late nineteenth century carry dates in only a few instances. One of the greatest problems hitherto was the dating of the First Imperial Egg, the matte white enameled egg lined with gold that opens to display a little golden hen within its golden yolk.

A major discovery in Fabergé studies has now been made by M. Lopato in the Central State Historical Archives of the USSR, where the files are kept concerning the imperial orders and commissions initi-

Viennese Reliquary, late nineteenth century, made of rock crystal mounted on a silver gilt and enamel stem. Crystal tabernacle encloses gilt and enamel Crucifixion scene. Note similarity of style to the Resurrection Egg.

Opposite: Danish Jubilee Egg, 1906. Whereabouts unknown.

Winter Egg, 1913. Bryan Ledbrook, Esq.

ated by the Court Minister of His Majesty's Cabinet. The information deduced from these archives shows that the First Imperial Egg was made in 1885 and presented at Easter of that year. Although no further information on this egg has been made available, the complete dossier of the second Imperial Easter Egg has been published by M. Lopato in the January 1984 *Apollo*. Starting on February 15, 1886, and ending on April 26 of the same year, the entries show that Fabergé was not totally free to execute his ideas, but first had to get approval from the Court Minister for various suggestions regarding the decoration of the Easter present. The file, "Regarding the manufacture of a hen of gold and rose diamonds, taking a sapphire out of a nest, made by Fabergé, and the payment of 2,986 Rubles 25 Kopecks for it," records the jeweler's queries and respective notes of approval or decisions by the assistant manager to the Cabinet. Here are Fabergé's questions and the Court Minister's answers to them:

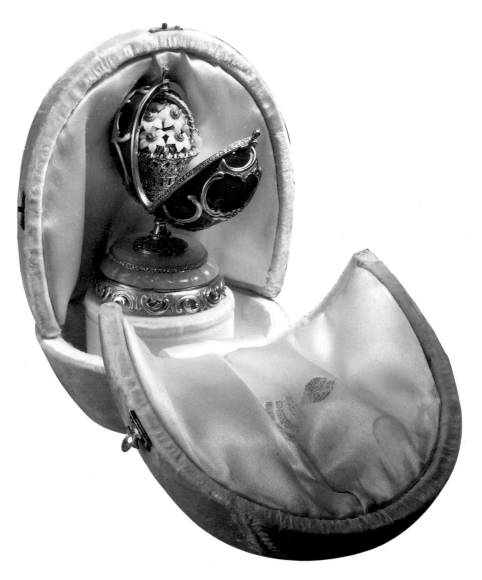

Above and opposite: Spring Flowers Egg, before 1899, by Perchin. THE FORBES Magazine Collection, New York.

Blue Enamel Ribbed Egg, before 1899, by Perchin. Private collection, Switzerland.

To manufacture a hen taking an egg out of a wicker basket it is necessary to know:

Q   When the piece must be ready?
A   It is preferable to have it finished by Easter, but not if this will be detrimental to the quality.
Q   Whether the hen must be made of silver only or set with roses [rose diamonds]?
A   It must be made of gold without roses.
Q   Whether the egg should be loose or fastened to the beak?
A   It must be loose. (15 February 1886)

By order of the Minister, the commission for a hen taking an egg out of a wicker basket, so that the hen could be made of metal without roses. Meanwhile the jeweller Fabergé, while carrying out this commission, stated that the hen should be set with [diamond] roses, otherwise it would not be beautiful and would look like a bronze one.

> Reported to the Minister.
> Agreed to set the hen with roses.
> (signed) N. Petrov.

This Easter gift, which unfortunately is now lost, was sent on April 2, 1886 by a courier to Tsarskoe Selo, where the Imperial Family was staying at the time.

Later, in the dossier recording the commission for the 1889 Easter egg (stock 468, inventory 7, file 372), a list of all Easter presents made by Fabergé since 1885 is given:

For the presents of His Majesty on Easter day the following were manufactured:

1885   *Easter egg of white enamel, the crown is set with rubies, diamonds and roses*
4,151 Rubles (including 2 ruby eggs—2,700 Rubles)
1886   *The hen taking a sapphire egg out of the wicker basket*
2,986 Rubles (including the sapphire—1,800 Rubles)
1887   *Easter egg with a clock decorated with brilliants, sapphires and roses*
2,160 Rubles
1888   *Angel pulling a chariot with an egg—1,500 Rubles; angel with a clock in a gold egg—600 Rubles*
1889   *Pearl egg—981 Rubles*
All these are made by the jeweller Fabergé

February 1889

Unfortunately the descriptions are so short that it is difficult to trace the corresponding objects which, apart from the First Imperial Egg and the 1887 Serpent Clock Egg, seem to be lost. Although the manufacture of an "egg with an emerald" is recorded for 1890, its whereabouts is unknown. But there is better luck with the payment of 4,500 Rubles made on April 24, 1891, for the gold-mounted blood jasper egg in the Louis XV style with the model of the cruiser *Pamyat Azova*. We know that this egg is now in the Armory Museum of the Kremlin in Moscow. The published material about the imperial Easter presents stops with this 1891 Easter egg. A more comprehensive study of the archival material would undoubtedly turn up more precise information, including facts regarding the later eggs, their dating, costs, and decoration.

The first Easter eggs bearing a date as part of the decoration are the Caucasus Egg of 1893, followed by the Renaissance Egg of 1894. The eggs made after 1894 which are undated were related to a specific year by means of comparison or interpretation. The surprises enclosed in them often commemorate an event or jubilee of a determinable date. Other dates obviously depend very much on scholarly interpretation, and from time to time, when new evidence is unearthed by research, the chronological order undergoes a revision. For example, this occurred in the dating of the Easter egg containing the miniature model of the Gatchina Palace, now in the Walters Art Gallery, Baltimore. This egg was exhibited in 1902 at the Charity Exhibition in St. Petersburg and was mentioned in an article in the review *Niva, The Illustrated Journal of Literature and Contemporary Life,* in March 1902. Since Easter fell on April 14 in 1902, it can be presumed that this egg was presented before 1902, possibly at Easter in 1901.

It may also be suggested that the Danish Jubilee Egg, which is not recorded in the archives for the hitherto attributed date of 1888 and which stylistically does not fit into the series of early eggs, dates from 1906. King Christian IX of Denmark died on January 29, 1906. The egg, decorated with the Danish heraldic lions and the Order of the Elephant, has as its surprise a miniature portrait of the king. Nicholas II may well have presented this egg to the Dowager Empress Marie in memory of her father at Easter 1906.

Until the 1970s, objects by Fabergé were generally considered in relation to the art of the fin de siècle or Edwardian era. But recently authors have concentrated on tracing Fabergé's inspiration from the art-historical viewpoint. With regard to the Imperial Easter Eggs it is, of course, especially fascinating to discover those objects that obviously inspired Fabergé's creations.

This is the case with the 1894 Renaissance Egg, which was inspired by the Le Roy casket in the Dresden Green Vaults, or the 1908 Peacock Egg, inspired by the peacock automaton made by James Cox that is still kept in the Hermitage Museum. The 1903 Peter the Great Egg owes its idea to a rococo *nécessaire* which had once belonged to the Empress Elizabeth Petrovna and is now in the Hermitage Treasury. This list could continue with the 1906 Swan Egg, which was clearly inspired by the swan automaton by James Cox, exhibited at the 1867 Paris International Exhibition. The 1887 Serpent Clock Egg, as well as the Duchess of Marlborough Egg, finds its predecessors in neoclassical mantel clocks such as those supplied by the *marchand-mercier*

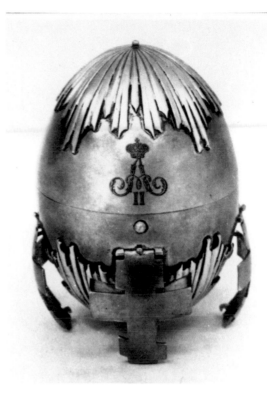

Parcel-gilt Silver Easter Egg, by Joseph Nordberg, made of silver and enamel bearing the monogram of Czar Alexander II, auctioned at Christie's London.

Simon-Philippe Poirier to Madame du Barry and to the French court about 1770.

All these parallels clearly show that Fabergé was a true representative of the period of historicism and eclecticism prevailing at the time. The difference between him and other contemporary jewelers such as Reinhold Vasters or Hermann Ratzersdorfer, who produced objects in style and quality that could have passed as articles from the Renaissance or earlier periods, is that Fabergé gave each piece his own distinctive cachet. He often accomplished this by slightly re-shaping an object, by transforming the elliptical Le Roy casket into an egg, for example, or by reducing the size of a piece or simply by dating it.

This typical Fabergé touch was the target of criticism by some of his contemporaries. R. Chanteclair, for instance, refers in his article on the 1900 Paris International Exhibition to the 1891 Azova Egg as follows:

> This small object, made by Holmstroem [a Fabergé workmaster] represents one year's work: we did not very much appreciate the patina, the external ornaments of the egg, which are slightly ex-aggerated in the combination of colors, and the rose-cut dia-monds in the centers of the rococo scrolls. As Monsieur Fabergé remains a true admirer of the French styles, we think he could eas-ily have chosen among each of these some ornamentations which are less known, but equally decorative.

Obviously, Fabergé preferred not to make an out-and-out copy of an eighteenth-century piece but rather to fashion an object in his personal style, inspired by a historical item.

Although the work of detecting antecedents for Fabergé objects, and for the Easter eggs in particular, might have surprising results, it can be said that the majority of the Easter eggs are original in style.

A strong influence on the style that characterizes objects by Fabergé was the *Mir Iskusstva* (World of Art) movement. Founded in 1898, *Mir Iskusstva* was an association of artists and writers, among them Serge Diaghilev, Alexandre Benois, Konstantin Somov, and Leon Bakst, who had started a magazine bearing the association's name. Its aim was twofold: to promote a national art, at that time guided by the Pan-Slavonic spirit, and to establish links with the rest of European art, particularly the progressive French movements, while reviving the artistic and cultural traditions of eighteenth- and early nineteenth-century Russia. It is known that Alexandre Benois, who was a stage designer for the Ballets Russes, also designed objects for Fabergé. The design of the 1905 Colonnade Easter Egg has been attributed to Benois. The putti for this egg derive from Eisen's eighteenth-century illustrations from *Les Baisers* of Claude-Joseph Dorat—but they are only one element in the composition of an object which, on the whole, can be recognized as an original Fabergé piece.

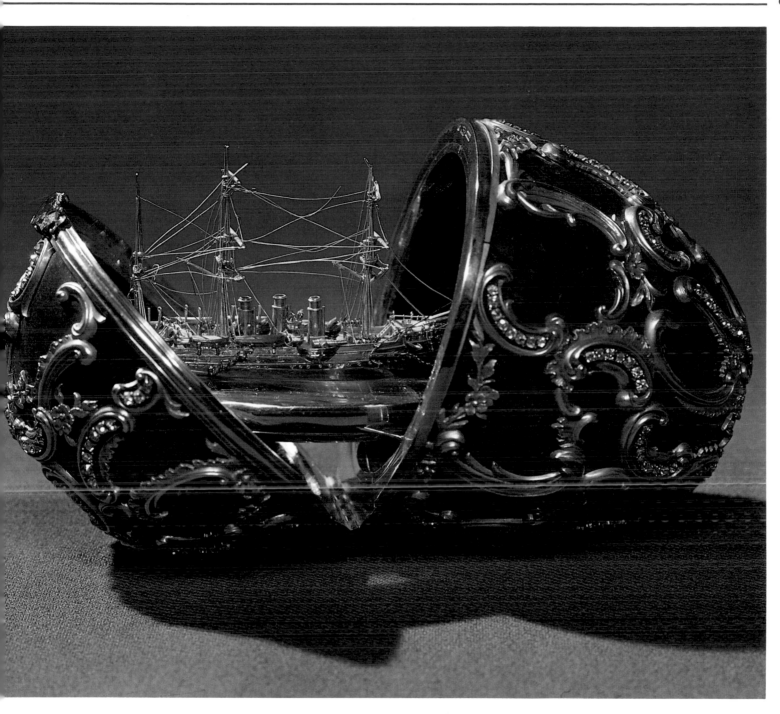

Azova Egg, 1891, by Perchin. Armory Museum, State Museums of the Moscow Kremlin.

Similarly, other Easter eggs have as their source historical motifs which were then developed into a unique Fabergé creation by combining various ornaments into a new style. Such is the case of the 1897 Coronation Egg, where the design of the exterior was inspired by the coronation robes of gold cloth embellished with imperial eagles, or of the 1912 Napoleonic Egg, where *empire* motifs are incorporated in the design.

Although rarely seen in Fabergé's general oeuvre, the Art Nouveau style is also represented by several Easter eggs: the 1898 Lilies of the Valley Egg, the 1899 Pansy Egg, and the Clover Egg, which can be dated about 1902. The latter is of a particularly fine quality with its net of clover leaves made of translucent enamel and precious stones.

Other eggs are in a style that can be characterized as specifically Fabergé. They do not follow the usual sources of inspiration recognized by his contemporaries. Such is the case with the 1914 Mosaic Egg. Encased in a gold-mounted platinum network partially pavé-set with diamonds and colored gems, it has five oval panels decorated with flower motifs in a mosaic-like technique. It was designed by Alma Klee, the daughter of the Fabergé workmaster Knut Oskar Pihl. The inspiration for this very unusual and delicate decoration for an egg came from her mother-in-law's petit point embroidery. The mosaic network actually gives a pointillistic effect. Alma Klee, a talented artist, also designed the 1913 Winter Egg, whose diamond-frosted shell contains a basket of flowers.

The concept of the imperial Easter present in the form of an egg that opened implied that it should contain a surprise. Traditionally, small jewels or miniature Easter eggs were concealed in these egg-shaped offerings as delightful surprises. In the later eggs, Fabergé's inventiveness was concentrated more and more on the art of creating unusual surprises. Miniature portraits of members of the Imperial Family in jeweled frames were often tucked away within an egg, or sometimes a tiny but meticulously detailed painting with a view of an imperial residence or palace was discovered. Two eggs open to display actual miniature models of palaces inside: the Gatchina Palace, a residence of the Dowager Empress near St. Petersburg, is rendered complete down to the flag flying from a turret in an egg probably made in 1901. The Easter egg given in 1908 to Empress Alexandra Feodorovna conceals a model of the Alexander Palace, the residence of the Czar's family in Tsarskoe Selo. Monuments, like the statue of Peter the Great by Falconet or that of Alexander III by Trubetzkoi, were replicated in miniature in the 1903 and 1910 eggs, as were the cruiser *Pamyat Azova,* on which Nicholas II had toured the world, and the Imperial yacht *Standart* in the 1891 and 1909 eggs.

The creation of the surprise for the 1897 Coronation Egg is well recorded as one of the more astonishing masterpieces from the House of Fabergé. In this case the surprise was a miniature replica in gold and enamel of the imperial coach used in 1896 for the coronation of Nicholas II and Empress Alexandra in Moscow. All details are faithfully copied from the original and include engraved rock crystal windows as well as two steps which can be let down when the coach doors are opened. This model was made by George Stein, who had been a master carriage builder and later an engraver with Fabergé. Known for his precise hand and keen eye for the minutest detail, Stein spent about fifteen months working on this tiny but perfectly articulated carriage.

Although the egg itself is signed by the chief workmaster, Michael Perchin, Henrik Wigström, his assistant and after 1903 his successor, was involved in the creation of this surprise, supervising the enameling. Wigström's daughter recalls going with her father to the imperial stables to check the exact shade of red on the seat of the coronation coach. The tiny gold model was then about to be enameled and he wanted to compare his shade of strawberry red with the original upholstery.

A similar toylike miniature replica is the surprise in the 1901 Trans-Siberian Railway Egg. This is a train comprised of engine, tender, and five coaches, the details of which were greatly admired at the 1902 Exhibition in St. Petersburg, as mentioned in the magazine *Niva*.

The automata represent a special category of Easter egg surprises. They seemed to appeal especially to Fabergé's inventiveness. There are six Easter eggs known with automata, excluding the more or less elaborate egg-shaped clocks: the 1900 Cuckoo Egg, the 1906 Swan Egg, the 1908 Peacock Egg, the 1911 Orange Tree Egg, and the Pine Cone and Chanticleer Eggs.

The so-called Cuckoo Egg, whose surprise is in fact not a cuckoo but a rooster, is in the shape of a clock decorated in an original style blending baroque and Moorish elements. The surprise is a singing bird mechanism that is independent of the clock movement. The bird automaton is released by pushing a button. The openwork cover on the top of the egg springs up to reveal a cockerel decorated with real feathers! Similar to the bird automata of early nineteenth-century Swiss origin, the cockerel opens its beak and moves its wings rhythmically while the sound of birdsong can be heard, produced by miniature bellows within the works.

A similar automaton is concealed within the Chanticleer Egg. However, closer examination shows that its mechanism is much more complicated. In fact, even externally, the Chanticleer Egg is more elaborate, its enameled surface set with pearls. The clock and the automaton here are connected, so that the crowing cockerel appears automatically on the hour. The movements of the beak and wings are synchronized with the crowing. In the book *Automata* by A. Chapuis and E. Droz, a technical report on the various movements of the complicated mechanism of the chanticleer is given: it consists of three separate trains, two of which are further subdivided, while three independent barrels actuate five mechanisms.

Silver Anniversary Egg, 1892, by Perchin. The Hillwood Museum, Washington, D.C.

Caucasus Egg, 1893, by Perchin. The Matilda Geddings Gray Foundation Collection, New Orleans.

While the singing bird automaton in the 1911 Orange Tree Egg is similar to the one in the Cuckoo Egg, a highly sophisticated mechanism was used for the surprise of the 1906 Swan Egg. The eggshell opens to reveal a swan swimming on a miniature lake made of an aquamarine with applied gold water lilies. When wound up under one wing the bird, which is less than two inches long, starts to glide, moving its webbed feet. It wags its tail characteristically, and the head and arched neck are proudly raised and then lowered. The wings open and spread to display each set of feathers separately.

A similar bird automaton is the surprise in the 1908 Peacock Egg,

obviously inspired by James Cox's famous peacock automaton in the Hermitage. When wound up and placed on a flat surface, the enameled gold bird struts proudly about, placing one leg carefully before the other, moving its head and at intervals spreading and closing its spectacular tail. The workmaster Dorofeev, a self-taught mechanic, is said to have worked on this automaton for three years.

The surprise in the Pine Cone Egg (possibly 1900) is an automated elephant. When it is wound, the elephant slowly advances, shifting its weight cumbrously from one side to the other, turning its head and switching its tail. Technically the movements are identical with the ones of the rhinoceros automaton illustrated on page 18.

Above: Rosebud Egg, 1895. Whereabouts unknown.

Opposite: Renaissance Egg, 1894, by Perchin. The FORBES Magazine Collection, New York.

Overleaf: Danish Palace Egg, 1895, by Perchin. The Matilda Geddings Gray Foundation Collection, New Orleans.

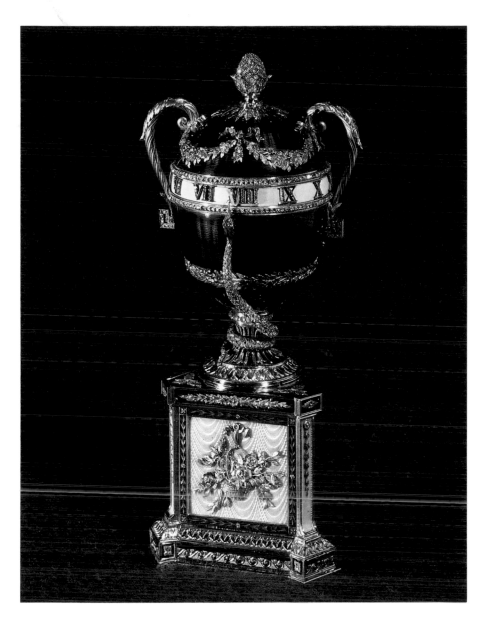

Blue Serpent Clock Egg, 1887, by Perchin. Private collection, Switzerland.

Opposite: Egg with Revolving Miniatures, 1896, by Perchin. Virginia Museum of Fine Arts, Richmond.

Another automaton, which has not hitherto been connected with an Easter egg surprise, is the little Sedan Chair, in which Empress Catherine the Great is carried by two court blackamoors. The Empress is realistically represented wearing the crown and ermine-trimmed imperial robes, enameled in translucent colors. The sedan chair has tiny rock crystal windows and is beautifully chased and engraved in varicolored gold, decorated with the imperial eagle. The men carrying the chair wear turbans and are dressed in brilliant liveries of red enamel. When the clockwork mechanism is wound, the two court lackeys start to walk, slowly moving their legs while the chair is propelled by two tiny wheels connected to the mechanism.

This marvelous toy was made in the workshop of Henrik Wigström and bears the stamped signature *Fabergé* in Latin characters. The inspiration for this very amusing object apparently derives from a

Coronation Egg, 1897, by Perchin and Wigström. The FORBES Magazine Collection, New York.

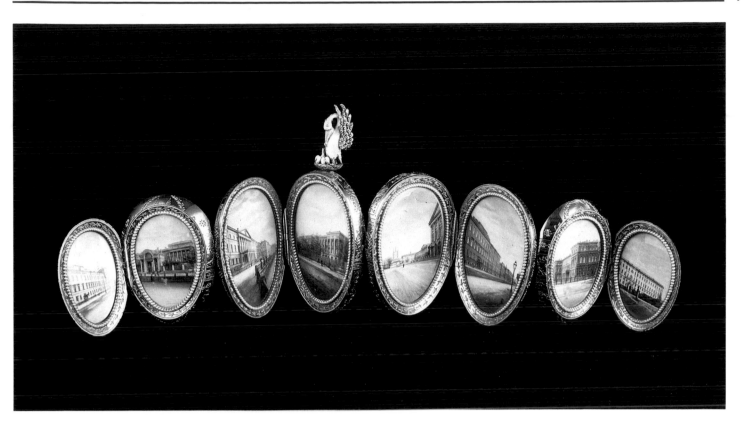

Above: The Pelican Egg surprise is a series of miniatures of institutions of which the dowager empress was patron.

Left: Pelican Egg, 1897, by Perchin. Virginia Museum of Fine Arts, Richmond.

Watercolor drawing with the design for an Easter egg by Hugo Oeberg, from the Fabergé Archives. Initialed "A. F." (Agathon Fabergé).

Opposite: Lilies of the Valley Egg, 1898, by Perchin. The FORBES Magazine Collection, New York.

Right: Madonna Lily Egg, 1899, by Perchin. Armory Museum, State Museums of the Moscow Kremlin.

similar sedan chair automaton dating back to the eighteenth century which is exhibited in the Hermitage.

The imperial provenance and the indication that this sedan chair was made as a surprise for an Easter egg were recently discovered in a letter written by the Empress Marie Feodorovna to her sister, Queen Alexandra of England, and published with the kind permission of H. R. H. Princess Eugenie of Greece and Denmark. The letter, dated April 8, 1914, is written in Danish, a language often used by the Empress, who was born a Danish princess:

> From Nicky I have good news, thank God. They are happy to be in L[ivadia], and enjoy the beautiful weather, and have a little more freedom, the poor things. He wrote me a most charming letter and presented me with a most beautiful Easter egg. Fabergé brought it to me himself. It is a true *chef-d'oeuvre,* in pink enamel and inside a *porte-chaise* carried by two blackamoors with Empress Catherine in it wearing a little crown on her head. You wind it, and then the blackamoors walk: it is an unbelievably beautiful and superbly fine piece of work. Fabergé is the greatest genius of our time, I also told him: "vous êtes un génie incomparable."

The pink enamel Easter egg mentioned above is decorated with panels *en grisaille* that depict the seasons. Not until the letter from the Dowager Empress to her sister was disclosed recently was the empty Grisaille Egg linked to the sedan chair. This egg, which now

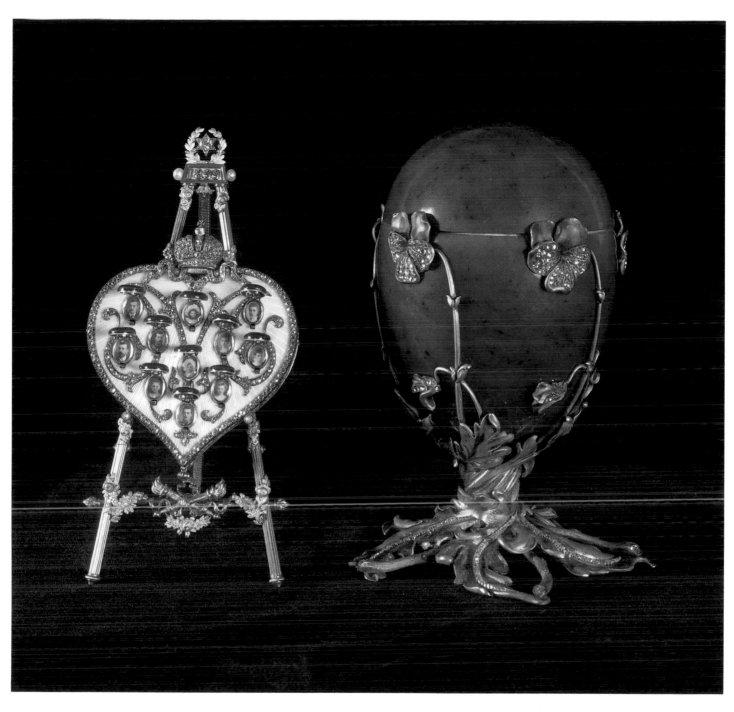

Pansy Egg, 1899, by Perchin. Its surprise was eleven miniature portraits mounted
on a heart. Private collection, U.S.A.

Inside the Cuckoo Egg this automaton activates the singing bird.

Opposite: Cuckoo Egg, 1900, by Perchin. Mr. and Mrs. Bernard S. Soloman, Los Angeles.

Below: Pine Cone Egg, possibly 1900, by Perchin. Private collection, U.S.A.

Trans-Siberian Railway Egg, 1901, by Perchin. Armory Museum, State Museums of the Moscow Kremlin.

Apple Blossom Egg, possibly 1901, by Perchin. Private collection, U.S.A.

Opposite: Clover Egg, 1902, by Perchin. Armory Museum, State Museums of the Moscow Kremlin.

might more appropriately be called the Catherine the Great Egg, is in the Marjorie Merriweather Post Collection at Hillwood. It bears the date 1914 and the monogram of Marie Feodorovna under portrait diamonds top and bottom.

The 1914 Grisaille Egg and its dissociated surprise give an example of how the Imperial Collection was dispersed following the Revolution. Most of the Imperial Easter Eggs are scattered over the world in various collections.

To trace the whereabouts of these incomparable Easter gifts between 1917 and 1927 is very difficult. For various reasons—political, financial, or perhaps merely due to lack of interest—the subject of the Fabergé pieces from the Imperial Collections was always left untouched. Contemporary Soviet sources are completely insensitive to the question of how the imperial and other collections of Fabergé objects were dispersed.

Only one egg, the 1916 Cross of St. George Egg, left Russia with its proper owner, the Dowager Empress Marie. It accompanied her into exile when she left the Crimea for England in April 1919 and later settled at Hvidøre, her villa outside Copenhagen in her native Denmark. The Empress managed to take with her a large number of her jewels and valuables. After her death in 1928, and after disputes over

Gatchina Palace Egg, before 1902, by
Perchin. The Walters Art Gallery, Baltimore.

Opposite: Peter the Great Egg, 1903, by
Perchin. Virginia Museum of Fine Arts,
Richmond.

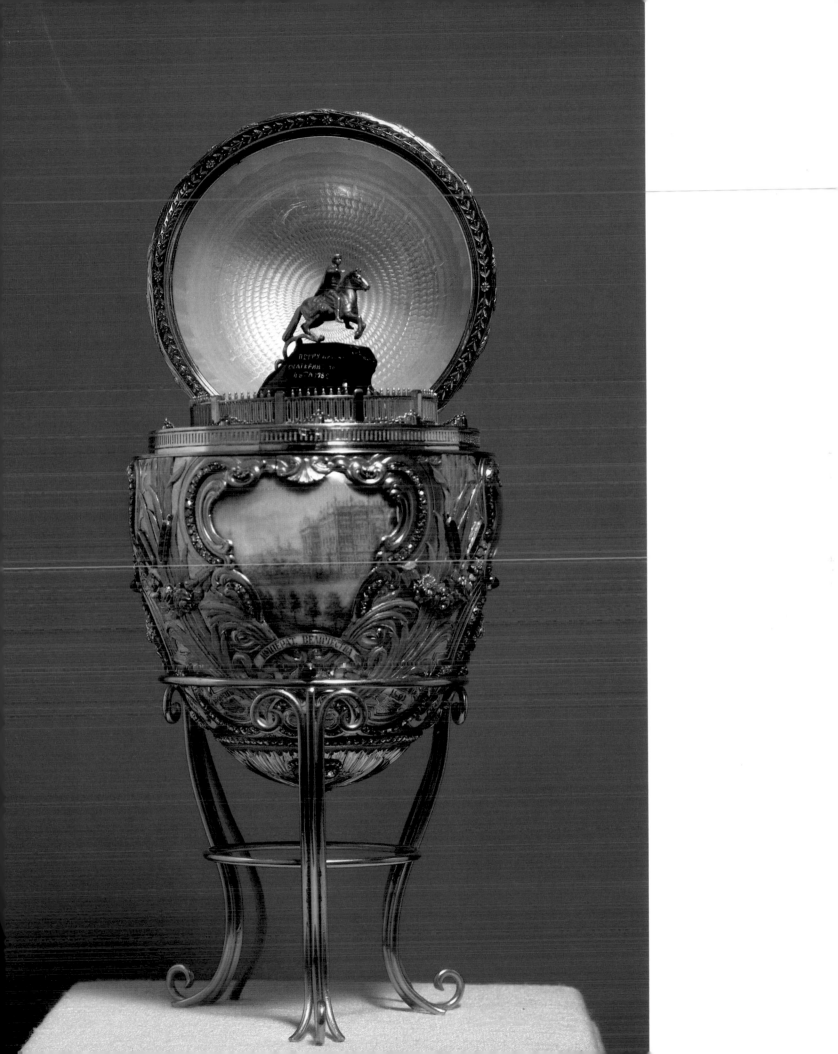

Chanticleer Egg, possibly 1903, by Perchin. The FORBES Magazine Collection, New York.

Right: Chanticleer Egg, detail. The beautiful little chanticleer appears on the hour, when the openwork cover springs up. As it crows, its wings and beak move.

Above: Egg with Love Trophies, 1905. Private collection, U.S.A.

Left: Uspensky Cathedral Egg, 1904. Armory Museum, State Museums of the Moscow Kremlin.

Opposite: Colonnade Egg, 1905, by Wigström. Royal Collection, England.

Swan Egg, 1906. Heirs of the late Maurice Sandoz, Switzerland.

Left: Rose Trellis Egg, 1907, by Wigström. The Walters Art Gallery, Baltimore.

Alexander Palace Egg, 1908, by Wigström.
Armory Museum, State Museums of the
Moscow Kremlin.

Peacock Egg, 1908, by Wigström. Heirs of the late Maurice Sandoz, Switzerland.

the inheritance, they were brought to England where they were sold by the London jewelers Hennel & Sons Ltd., fetching £350,000.

One of the few items kept by the children of the Empress was the Cross of St. George Egg, perhaps for reasons of sentiment. Not until 1961 was it sold on behalf of her grandson, Prince Vassily Romanov, and it was later acquired for the FORBES Magazine Collection. With the exception of this egg, the remaining fifty-three were left in the imperial residences after the Czar and his family were taken to Ekaterinburg and the Dowager Empress had gone into exile. The expropriation of private property was instituted by the Soviets in 1917. All the residences, collections, and belongings of the Imperial Family were now considered the property of the people. Although there was much damage caused by revolutionary activities, Lenin and his government wanted to conserve historical monuments as examples of a pre-Revolutionary past.

Accounts of what happened to the imperial property after November 1917 are meager. In 1919 and 1923, Alexander Polovtsoff and George Lukomskij, both of whom had been curators of imperial

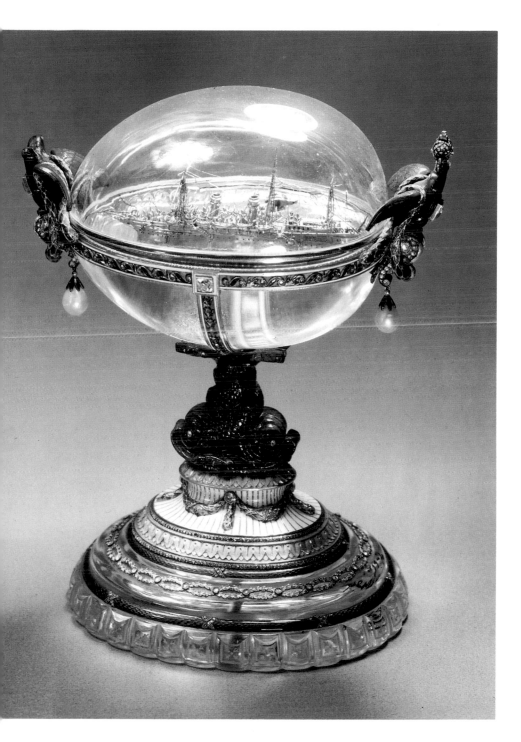

Alexander III Commemorative Egg, 1904.
Whereabouts unknown.

Left: Standart Egg, 1909, by Wigström.
Armory Museum, State Museums of the
Moscow Kremlin.

Alexander III Equestrian Egg, 1910. Armory Museum, State Museums of the Moscow Kremlin.

Below: Fifteenth Anniversary Egg, 1911. The FORBES Magazine Collection, New York.

Opposite: Orange Tree Egg, 1911. The FORBES Magazine Collection, New York.

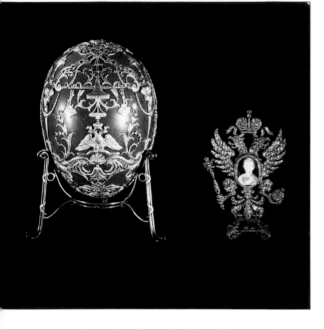

Czarevitch Egg, 1912, by Wigström. Virginia Museum of Fine Arts, Richmond.

Right: Napoleonic Egg, 1912, by Wigström. The Matilda Geddings Gray Foundation Collection, New Orleans.

Romanov Tercentenary Egg, 1913, by
Wigström. Armory Museum, State
Museums of the Moscow Kremlin.

palaces until the end of 1918, published descriptions of the confiscatory events. Polovtsoff was responsible for the Gatchina Palace; Lukomskij was in charge of the palaces in Tsarskoe Selo including the Alexander Palace, the last residence of the Imperial Family. Lukomskij gives an interesting account of his work on the conservation of the palace. He mentions that Lunacharsky, the Commissar for Cultural Affairs, was for a time opposed to the registration of items of historical interest and that he decreed that no objects which a member of the family of the last Czar had touched could ever be historically valuable.

Despite the Commissar's opposition, careful inventories of the imperial palaces were made and all the collections catalogued. An example is the catalogue of the crown jewels which was undertaken between 1921 and 1923 and published in A. E. Fersman's *Les Joyaux du Trésor de Russie*. Agathon Fabergé, the second son of Carl and a well-known gemmologist, then belonged to a group of scientists who catalogued not only the imperial regalia, but also the jewels and precious objects which had belonged to the Imperial Family. Among all

Grisaille Pin, made of gold, enamel, and diamonds with a design after Boucher representing winter, identical to one of the eight grisaille enamels painted by Vassily Zuiev that decorate the Catherine the Great (Grisaille) Egg.

Mosaic Egg, 1914. Royal Collection, England.

Catherine the Great (Grisaille) Egg, 1914, by Wigström. The Hillwood Museum,
Washington, D.C.

The surprise of the 1914 Imperial Easter Egg was this miniature gold and enamel sedan chair with a figure of Catherine the Great borne by two liveried blackamoors. A small gold key winds the clockwork mechanism, enabling the men to walk naturalistically. The late Sir Charles Clore, London.

The underside of the sedan chair, stamped with the Fabergé and workmaster marks, shows how it operates.

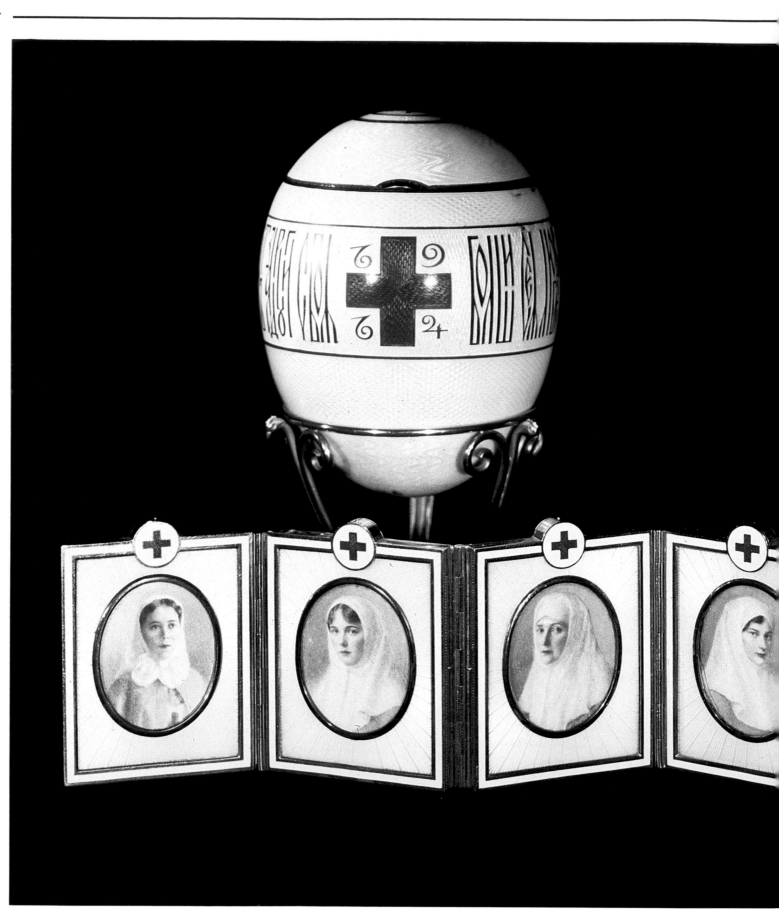

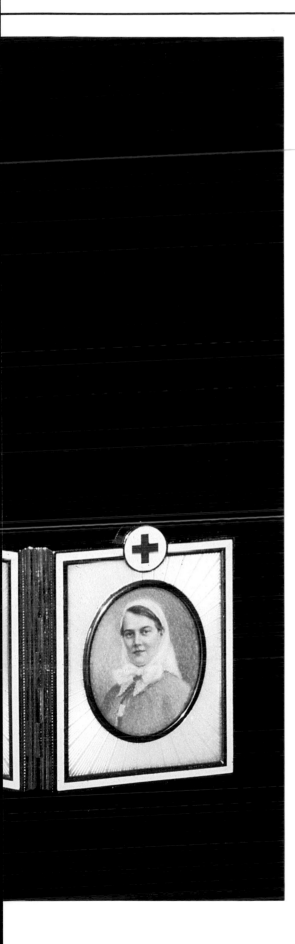

Red Cross Egg with Resurrection Triptych,
1915, by Wigström. The Cleveland
Museum of Art, India Early Minshall
Collection.

Left: Red Cross Egg with Portraits, 1915, by
Wigström. Virginia Museum of Fine Arts,
Richmond.

the possessions of Nicholas II, only two large necklaces, one made for the costume ball in 1898, the other of turquoise and diamonds, and a magnifying glass with a gold-mounted white enamel and nephrite handle (Nr. 297) are recorded as being by Fabergé. Sir Martin Conway, a British art historian who traveled through Russia in 1924, confirmed in his *Art Treasures in Soviet Russia* the Soviets' tendency to safeguard art.

In describing the private apartments of the Imperial Family, authors such as Lukomskij, Polovtsoff, and Conway never mention objects by Fabergé displayed in the rooms, although photographs taken before 1917 show picture frames, desk ornaments, and other typical Fabergé items. Obviously, art historians of the twenties looked at these rooms from a different point of view and judged the decor to be out of fashion. Conway reports on the Winter Palace: "Far more interesting than the State Apartments are the rooms in which the Czars actually lived. What they actually did was to hunt out some obscure set of small rooms in some remote corner of the huge building and to furnish them in the simplest, least tasteful and most bourgeois style of their day."

Lukomskij similarly describes the apartments in the Alexander Palace, which were partially decorated in the Art Nouveau style. An explanation for the disappearance of the Fabergé pieces can be found in his account that all valuables, including silver and other items made of precious metal, were collected after March 1918 and packed in boxes. They were sent to the Winter Palace for later transport to Moscow. Lukomskij mentions among the items "table-ornaments and Easter eggs," unfortunately without further details. What actually happened to this hoard of imperial valuables is not explained, although it seems that until Lenin's death in 1924 nothing had been sold and that the Soviet government did not at that time intend to sell art. Within a few months of Lenin's death, however, this policy was reversed.

As of 1925, contacts with art dealers were made by the Soviet government. Officials of the new government approached the Paris art dealer Germain Seligman, proposing sales in France, an offer which the dealer declined rather than risk offending the numerous and still influential Russian émigrés in that country.

The change in the Soviet policy officially occurred in 1927, on the eve of the first Five Year Plan. The first public sale took place in London at Christie's on March 16, 1927. This sale consisted of a portion of the crown jewels that had been carefully catalogued by the Soviets some years before. The sales catalogue states that the jewels had been "purchased by a syndicate in this country." The Soviet government, which needed Western currencies for financing their economy, had now started to sell art.

Apparently the money realized, from valuables collected not only from imperial residences but also from other private properties,

went by the high-sounding name of the "Foreign Currency Fund." Through the Antiquariat, a division of the Ministry of Foreign Trade, collectors, dealers, and diplomats were given the opportunity to buy art and museum pieces of all kinds in exchange for Western currencies. The most assiduous buyers at that time were Andrew Mellon, Calouste Goulbenkian, and Armand Hammer.

As already described, Dr. Hammer and Emanuel Snowman started to buy Fabergé pieces, with particular attention to the Imperial Easter Eggs. The eggs were acquired either from the Russian Antiquariat or, according to Hammer, in Berlin, where a number of eggs had been sent for sale. Hammer bought thirteen Imperial Easter Eggs: the 1885 First Imperial Egg, the 1893 Caucasus Egg, the 1894 Renaissance Egg, the 1895 Danish Palace Egg, the 1896 Egg With Revolving

Miniatures, the 1897 Pelican Egg, the 1899 Pansy Egg, the (possibly 1900) Pine Cone Egg, the 1906 Swan Egg, the 1912 Czarevitch Egg, the 1912 Napoleonic Egg, the 1914 Grisaille Egg, and the 1915 Red Cross Egg. Snowman acquired the 1887 Serpent Clock Egg, the 1897 Coronation Egg, the 1898 Lilies of the Valley Egg, the 1900 Cuckoo Egg, and the 1905 Colonnade Egg. The sedan chair with the miniature figure of Catherine the Great is recorded by A. K. Snowman as one of the first Fabergé pieces to have left Soviet Russia, and it was apparently already dissociated from its egg, which since 1931 has reposed in the collection of Mrs. Post.

Those eggs that were left unsold—one of them, the 1909 Standart Egg, had suffered damage, with the imperial crown broken off of the eagle finial—became the property of the Armory Museum of the Kremlin in Moscow. Exhibition catalogues today quote as the provenance: "Accessioned from the Foreign Currency Fund in 1927."

While the selling of Fabergé objects continued until the late 1930s, apparently most of the Imperial Easter Eggs were purchased at the inception of the new Soviet sales policy around 1927.

Based upon the recently discovered documents that record 1885 as the date of the First Imperial Egg, it can be ascertained that through 1916 fifty-four Imperial Eggs were made by Fabergé. Ten of these are still in the USSR, in the Armory Museum in Moscow. The majority of the others are now in the United States; some of them are kept anonymously in private collections and are rarely placed on view at exhibitions. The 1906 Danish Jubilee Egg and the 1904 Alexander III Commemorative Egg are known only from a photograph in an album made for Fabergé's London branch before 1915. While the album, published by Bainbridge in his *Connoisseur* articles of 1934, is still in the archives of the Fabergé family, the eggs themselves have not yet been found.

Other recorded eggs, known from photographs but presently not located, are the 1895 Rosebud Egg and the 1913 Winter Egg. The Rosebud Egg is said to have been destroyed or badly damaged by its owner during the 1930s. The Winter Egg was sold at public auction in 1949 as part of the collection of Sir Bernard Eckstein and surfaced later as the property of Bryan Ledbrook. As of the 1960s it seems to have disappeared—although, it is hoped, not forever.

The idea of undiscovered or hidden Imperial Easter Eggs gives the history of Fabergé objects another fascinating dimension. There might be imperial treasures tucked away in bank vaults or just standing on an apartment mantelpiece somewhere without their owners' having an inkling of the trinkets' historical and financial value. With some clever detective work, perhaps heretofore unrecorded Imperial Easter Eggs might be found, as well as those known only from photographs, so that eventually almost all of Fabergé's greatest masterpieces will be accounted for.

Cross of St. George Egg, 1916, with Czar Nicholas II miniature, The FORBES Magazine Collection, New York.

Czarina Alexandra and Czar Nicholas II, portrayed on the Coronation Egg.

Above: Fifteenth Anniversary Egg, 1911. The FORBES Magazine Collection, New York.

Czarevitch Alexis.

The Imperial Easter Egg of 1911: Russia During the Reign of Nicholas II

Marilyn Pfeifer Swezey

Grand Duchess Olga.

Grand Duchess Tatiana.

Grand Duchess Marie.

Grand Duchess Anastasia.

Russian Easter in 1911 fell on Sunday, April 23. On that day, as was his yearly custom, Czar Nicholas II presented his wife, Alexandra, with an especially designed egg from Fabergé. What must have been their surprise to see illustrated on it scenes from their reign of the past fifteen years! The nine superb miniatures on the Fifteenth Anniversary Egg were painted by Vassily Zuiev from photographs and drawings of the time. These small paintings are rare illustrations of historical events almost unknown or forgotten today, and revealing something of the enormous growth of Russia during those years.

Many contemporary observers, both native and foreign, noted the climate of progress in Russia before 1917. One of them was an American, Gilbert Grosvenor of the *National Geographic,* who in 1914 described the country as "a youth among the nations . . . because she never had a chance to grow until recent years." The period to which he alluded began with the liberation of some 50 million serfs by the proclamation in 1861 of Alexander II, the grandfather of Nicholas II. Russia's development in almost every sphere of national life boded well for the future. Among the many successful private businesses that grew and flourished in the general atmosphere of technical and economic progress was the firm of Fabergé.

However, these improved times were clouded by terrorist opposition to the government, to all of its reforms and, in fact, to the monarchy itself. The government was unable to combat this terrorism with sufficient force to prevent its most dire consequences. Alexander II was assassinated by political terrorists in March 1881 not long before he intended to sign a plan for a constitution. Terrorists also shortened the life of Alexander III, who died in 1894 at the age of forty-nine as a result of an injury sustained when the imperial train was bombed near Kharkov in October 1888. The train was derailed, causing the roof of the dining car, where the Czar and his family were finishing a meal, to cave in. Alexander III was a giant of a man: with enormous strength he simply lifted the roof onto his shoulders and

The Huis ten Bosch, The Hague.

held it long enough for his wife and children to escape unhurt. But as a result of this tremendous exertion, the Czar developed the kidney disease which finally killed him.

By 1911 the government seemed to have survived the various political attacks surrounding the revolution of 1905, and following the proclamation of a manifesto which granted full civil liberties and established a State Duma with legislative powers, Russia entered a final period of remarkable economic, social, and artistic development.

"May this day mark the rebirth of Russia's best forces," concluded the Czar in his speech opening the Duma on April 27, 1906. Nearly 200 of the 450 delegates elected to the First Duma were semi-literate peasants, while the rest were intellectuals of the educated classes. Many were socialist revolutionaries, unappeasable enemies of the government. The Emperor, knowing this, made an appeal for mutual service to the fatherland. An official photograph was taken of the scene in the Throne Room, St. George's Hall, in the Winter Palace, and it is this picture that was reproduced in miniature and in color by Vassily Zuiev for the Imperial Easter Egg of 1911.

The establishment of the Duma was a major step toward constitutional government and represented the great hope of many for political growth and development. But for the constant struggle with radical socialist revolutionaries, whose aim was to undermine both the monarchy and the constitutionalists, leaders such as Michael

First Peace Conference at The Hague, 1899.

Below: Unveiling of the statue of Peter the Great at Riga.

Rodzianko, Prince Eugene Troubetskoi, Paul Miliukov, and Alexander Guchkov might have succeeded in changing Russia from an autocracy to a genuine constitutional monarchy.

Nicholas II, however, consistently reaffirmed his father's belief in political autocracy and as Emperor remained the final arbiter of all affairs of state, able to dissolve the Duma when its members became too demanding. What many may never have understood, however, was that Nicholas's own view of his role was more religious than political. A devout member of the Orthodox Church, Nicholas believed that he had inherited a profound responsibility to God for the welfare of his people.

While Peter the Great had secularized the concept of the Czar, the Orthodox Church continued to regard the sovereign—in the tradition of the Byzantine emperors—as the anointed of God with a sacred responsibility of service to the Russian people. "As there is no power higher, so there is no power on earth more arduous than the power of Czar, no burden so wearisome as the duty of Czar," the Metropolitan of Moscow told the young Nicholas at his coronation in 1896, in the Uspensky Cathedral in the Kremlin.

The crown itself symbolized not only the honor and glory of this exalted office but the heavy burden of service to the nation; it weighed nine pounds. As it rested on Nicholas's brow it pressed on the very spot where a Japanese fanatic had stabbed him a few years earlier, during a trip to the Far East, and caused him an excruciating

Photograph of the opening of the Duma in the Throne Room.

Right: The Throne Room of the Winter Palace.

Opposite: The moment of coronation.

headache which he had to bear throughout the long ceremonies and festivities. As Nicholas took the crown and placed it on his brow, the Metropolitan of St. Petersburg turned to him saying that it was Christ Himself who was irrevocably crowning him as the ruling authority over his people. It was this deep religious conviction with which Nicholas had assumed the burden of power that much later was the real basis of his reluctance to accept a constitutional government in its fullest sense.

The actual moment of the crowning as well as other scenes of the coronation were recorded by artists who were present in the Uspensky Cathedral—Valentin Serov was one of them—and it was from these historic watercolors that Zuiev reproduced the two scenes of the coronation on the 1911 egg.

The early years of the reign were characterized by idealism, hope, and the birth of a succession of daughters. Shortly after the coronation, the new young Czar, accompanied by his wife and their infant daughter, Olga, made a highly successful state visit to France, where he laid the cornerstone of the Alexander III Bridge in Paris. A symbol of the Franco-Russian alliance initiated by Alexander III, the bridge was a fitting memorial to the Russian Czar known as "The Peacemaker," but it was the personal charm and attractiveness of the

An artist's rendering of the ceremony inside the Cathedral.

young couple and their baby that won the heart of Paris during "Russian Week." The crowds were particularly taken by little Grand Duchess Olga and shouted "Vive la bébé!" as the open carriage was drawn through the streets of Paris. This visit must have done much to cement the successful alliance between the French republic and the Russian autocracy, which became, in fact, the cornerstone of Russian foreign policy. For Nicholas it was a commitment which Russia heroically honored in 1914 when Russian troops saved Paris from German attack by opening a second front at the Battle of Tannenberg.

While the relations of Russia with the West were good, those with the East were less so. The opening of the Trans-Siberian railway and the development of Siberian resources turned Russia's attention at the end of the century toward a "window on the Pacific." Here Russia came up against Japan—which in 1904 attacked the Russian fort at Port Arthur, starting the war that resulted in a series of defeats for Russia.

In the wake of the disastrous Russo-Japanese War and the intensification of political unrest by the socialist revolutionaries, the months that followed were a crucial turning point in Russian history. Following the uprising of January 1905, the Czar issued a directive promising to convene representatives of the people in an advisory capacity, and by April of the following year deputies had been elected to the First Duma. Revolutionary activity subsided and the reform movement begun by the government in 1861 was renewed.

One of the most successful of these government programs was the granting of private ownership of land to the peasantry, the purpose of which was to create an agricultural middle class of independent farmers. Altogether some 5 million peasant families took part in this program, and by 1913 Russia was able to supply the world with one quarter of its wheat. That year, it produced 200 million bushels more than did the United States.

Industrial growth in Russia between 1900 and 1913 closely resembled the growth that had taken place in the United States several decades earlier. During this period the textile industry, one of the oldest in Russia, grew from a scattering of small family businesses into huge industrial concerns employing a total of over 800,000 workers. The owners of more than half of Moscow's fifty largest industrial and trade companies were descendants of peasants who had undergone a great cultural change. While their grandfathers were often illiterate, and the next generation still followed the traditional way of life, the third generation, benefiting from an education, was not only cultivated but had become wealthy. Many of these rich industrialists were patrons of the arts—and of Fabergé—among them clients such as Barbara Kelch, who was heiress to a Siberian gold mining fortune. The support of these people was an important factor in the extraordinary cultural and artistic renaissance of the early 1900s.

The Czar himself was a patron of the arts to a greater extent than

Coronation procession to Uspensky Cathedral.

Diamond-framed roundels with dates of the Czar's wedding and the fifteenth anniversary of his coronation, FA/BFR/GE hidden in the festooned garlands.

is generally known. While his patronage of the decorative arts, and particularly of Fabergé, is well known, he was also a frequent financial contributor to such art journals as the *World of Art*, which was published for several years by Diaghilev and others, as well as to the Ballets Russes, which took Paris by storm in 1909. The first Peoples Palace in St. Petersburg was built in 1902, not by the Soviets but by Nicholas II at his own expense. One of the first of these cultural projects was the opening in 1895 of a museum of Russian fine arts and ethnic arts dedicated to Alexander III. Formerly the Mikhailovsky Palace, it exists almost intact today as the Russian Museum in Leningrad.

This was a uniquely creative period for the arts. Developments in painting, literature, and music directly influenced theater, ballet, and the decorative arts. At the Paris Exposition of 1900, several of the Imperial Easter Eggs created by Fabergé for the Empresses were exhibited publicly for the first time, and Fabergé was made a master of the Parisian Goldsmiths' Guild and was decorated with the Legion of Honor by the French government.

In intellectual circles, in addition to liberalism in a variety of forms, many of the intelligentsia were beginning to turn to religion

The opening of the Alexander III Bridge in Paris.

Ceremonies inaugurating the construction of the Alexander III Bridge.

The Alexander III Museum.

Canonization ceremonies for St. Seraphim.

Monument commemorating the bicentenary of the Battle of Poltava.

and the theology of the Orthodox Church. Nicholas II and his family were devout Christians, and during his reign the number of churches in Russia increased by about 10,000 and the monasteries by 250.

One of the most personally significant events for the Imperial Family during the first fifteen years of Nicholas's reign was the canonization of St. Seraphim of Sarov, in which they participated. The Emperor, along with the clergy, grand dukes, and bishops, bore the coffin to the cathedral at Sarov for the canonization ceremonies on July 19, 1903. An eighteenth-century hermit and monk, Seraphim was popularly associated with many miraculous healings even during his lifetime. A young grand duchess and one of the Empresses, the wife of Nicholas I, great-grandmother of Nicholas II, had both been healed through the prayers of St. Seraphim and it was Nicholas II who had initiated the proceedings toward canonization.

"All the time the Emperor was at Sarov," wrote Prince Volkonsky, vice-president of the Duma and later Deputy Minister of the Interior, "he moved about among the people and the attitude of the crowd towards him was very touching." Surrounded by these crowds who shared his own feelings, Nicholas experienced that sense of unity with his people so central to his concept of autocracy. "All that the Czar had seen and felt at Sarov," Prince Volkonsky continued in his description published many years later, "remained a deep and happy memory in his heart." The miniature painting of the Czar in the canonization procession, done from a widely distributed photograph, which was included on the Easter egg of 1911, must have had a special significance for the Czarina, who shared a deep devotion to St. Seraphim. During their stay in Sarov, she had prayed to St. Seraphim, asking for his intercession for a son, and in 1904 the Czarevitch Alexis was born.

It has been related that when the Czar arrived at Sarov for the canonization, a letter was handed to him that had been written by Father Seraphim in his lifetime to the "fourth Czar" to come to Sarov. Nicholas II was the fourth. It is said that the letter warned of the events of the Revolution and the destruction of Orthodox Russia, which the saint, who was also known for his gift of prophecy, had foreseen in his own lifetime. The Czar reportedly turned white when he read the letter, but he never revealed its contents. Interestingly, the date was July 17, exactly fifteen years before the execution of the Imperial Family by the revolutionaries on July 17, 1918.

In the chaos of the Revolution the promise of Russia's development as seen in these vignettes was swept away, but the true spirit of Russia, as symbolized by the egg itself, can never be extinguished.

Wartski and Fabergé

A. Kenneth Snowman

Reading through what follows, I am deeply conscious of the fact that my text dwells unrelentingly upon events surrounding and affecting my own firm and family. I should like, therefore, to make it clear to the reader that I was specifically asked to relate, in a mood of reminiscence, what I could recall of our own activities as they touched upon the world of Fabergé and have tried as faithfully as I could to comply, with only minimal discursions.

My maternal grandfather, Morris Wartski, ran his business, which had been established in 1865, in the small university town of Bangor in one of the most beautiful regions of North Wales. He spoke English, his native Polish, Russian, and after a few years, Welsh as well. The agricultural community, steeped as it was in the Old Testament, looked forward with pleasurable anticipation to the visits of this enormous, genial, ruddy-complexioned man whom they took to their hearts as some sort of prophet.

The firm in those days was an extremely modest enterprise located at 21 High Street and was principally concerned with the sale of jewelry and silver, both old and new. Despite the small scale of his activities, my grandfather employed as his attorney no less a personage than David Lloyd George, later to become one of Great Britain's most successful, charming, and devious prime ministers.

The business moved from Bangor to the neighboring seaside resort of Llandudno in 1907, and during the next year my father, Emanuel Snowman, joined it. In Llandudno in 1909, he married Morris Wartski's daughter Harriette, who had been born and brought up in Bangor. My father was then twenty-three years old and my mother nineteen.

It should be emphasized that Llandudno at this time was an extremely fashionable resort known as "the Naples of Wales," featuring its own resident orchestra, often conducted by personalities such as Sir Malcolm Sargent and visited by the most celebrated musicians in the land. The Grand Theatre, too, attracted the most distinguished actors and actresses of the day. No lady or gentleman would have contemplated being seen strolling after dinner on the Promenade or

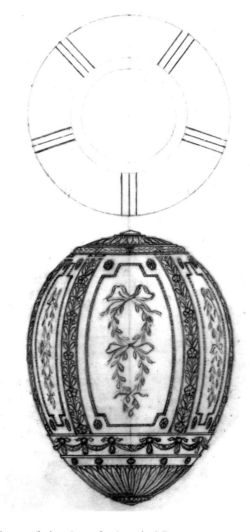

A pencil drawing of a jeweled Easter egg, from the Fabergé archives.

Opposite: The Twelve-panel Egg, 1899, by Perchin. Royal Collection, England.

The Bonbonnière Egg, 1903, by Perchin.
Private Collection.

along the splendid pier (which still exists) without full *tenue de soir*.

This Gaelic haven, which boasted two sandy beaches, naturally attracted the beau monde of nearby Cheshire and well-to-do tourists from the outlying industrial towns and cities who came with their families to relax by the sea. At that time neither the temptation nor even the possibility existed to fly off at the drop of a hat to a favorite European sun spot as we do now, and Llandudno, in common with many other seaside towns in Britain, flourished mightily. The firm rented showcases to display its wares in the two principal hotels, the Imperial and the Grand. I can still remember certain local characters in and around the town who were not so very far removed in flavor from the fictional inhabitants of Llareggub, that wondrous Welsh fantasy village of Dylan Thomas.

My father felt, however, that he did not want to bring up his family in Wales and he decided to return to London, where he had been born and had always lived and worked. In the teeth of a certain amount of opposition, this is exactly what he did, and in 1911 he opened a small shop at 13 New Bond Street. Several moves were made — to Garrick Street, the Quadrant Arcade off Regent Street, and

The Youssoupoff treasures, including
Fabergé jewelry and silver, spread out for
examination by Soviet officials in 1924.

subsequently to Regent Street. Then in 1975, five years after my father died, Wartski removed to our present premises in Grafton Street.

It was in 1925 that my father visited Russia for the first time in search of those art objects that were anathema to the Bolsheviks, representing as they did everything the new regime was required to despise. They were denounced at this time as playthings of the rich, which of course is exactly what those Fabergé confections were and still are; that is, in fact, why they were designed in the first place. The Soviets needed money to build up their economy and were glad to allow foreigners to come and purchase much of the vast treasure they had confiscated from the palaces and private collections.

In my book *Carl Fabergé, Goldsmith to the Imperial Court of Russia,* I have attempted to describe some of the difficulties that had to be overcome when transacting business with the Antiquariat authorities—how their fear of making blunders, combined with an aesthetic innocence in regard to the objects with which they had to deal, made progress very cumbersome and tiring.

Immense patience had to be exercised, and during the course of many visits, mainly to Moscow and St. Petersburg, my father learned how best to overcome these hazards. Consequently, over a period which extended until 1939, he was able to acquire marvelous old silver, eighteenth-century gold snuff boxes, porcelain, and jewels, quite apart from the objects by Carl Fabergé which have excited increasing interest and admiration since that time.

Among the most notable of the Easter eggs he was able to bring to England were those imperial examples known by the following names: Rosebud, Coronation, Lilies of the Valley, Cuckoo, Colonnade, Swan, Peacock, Orange Tree and Winter. As a result of Emanuel Snowman's first trips to Russia, and much careful selection and arduous negotiation, the *Times* of London on November 26, 1927, ran a long article under the heading "Russian Jewels, Royal Treasures sold by Soviet," part of which follows:

> Up to the time of the Revolution, many people in Russia, more particularly the Royal Family and some of the ancient nobility, were known to possess vast art treasures, not only pictures, but what are known as "objects of art" and bijouterie. . . . The fate of these things has been one of the mysteries to those outside Russia. The Russian State jewels were sold at Christie's a year or two ago. Quite recently a collection of beautiful things, about 80 in number—all of which could be comfortably stowed away in a Gladstone bag—has been brought to Paris by accredited members of the Soviet Government, and has been purchased by Mr. Emanuel Snowman (of Messrs. Wartski, the Court jewellers, of the Quadrant-arcade, Regent-street, and Llandudno). The Russian State jewels were the property of the State, but Mr. Snowman's "haul" includes many things that were the intimate personal property of various members of the unfortunate Royal Family. They are, from their beauty and exquisite workmanship, just the kind of things which would appeal to the aesthetic sense of the owners, things which the owners would have handled and treasured as personal belongings. They are nearly all modern, and are mostly the work of the famous Russian Court jeweller M. Fabergé, who is understood to be still in Russia, detained as a kind of expert and valuer to the Soviet Government.

Carl Fabergé had been dead seven years when these words were written; there is a confusion here with his son Agathon, who had indeed been helping to catalogue the Imperial Crown Jewels for the new regime.

When these examples from the Fabergé workshops arrived in London they were exhibited on our premises, and the late Queen Mary again took up with enthusiasm and intelligence the traditional role of connoisseur in these matters. Her Majesty acquired many of the most sensational items, which she added to the collection at Sandringham House in Norfolk, a collection that had been built up by King Edward VII and his beautiful Queen Alexandra, sister of the Czarina Marie Feodorovna. These important pieces selected by Queen Mary included three Easter eggs, two of them imperial, exquisite min-

Opposite: The Lilies of the Valley Egg being admired by Emanuel and Kenneth Snowman of Wartski, 1949.

iature models of furniture, gold presentation boxes, an elaborate rock crystal vase decorated in Renaissance revival taste, and an amusing stone *magot*, a little Oriental figure which gravely nods its head, moves its hands as in a blessing, and simultaneously and irreverently pokes its ruby tongue back and forth.

In 1949 when Henry Bainbridge, Fabergé's representative in London and a particularly agreeable man, wrote his life of Peter Carl Fabergé, we arranged a loan exhibition at Wartski in Regent Street to celebrate the publication. Eugène Fabergé, the eldest son of Carl, not only attended the opening but was, in his own engaging words, "the star." It was he who had each year delivered the Imperial Egg to the Czarina on Easter morning. This was the very first exhibition entirely devoted to the work of Fabergé, and both King George and the Queen lent personal possessions of which they were particularly fond.

In 1953, to celebrate the Coronation of Queen Elizabeth II, we mounted another Fabergé exhibition. Sir Sacheverell Sitwell began the foreword to our catalogue thus:

> June, the most beautiful month in the English calendar, has been chosen for the Coronation of Queen Elizabeth II, and it is a summer which we will all remember for that reason. Among its lesser events, many people may recall this exhibition of Fabergé objects from the Sandringham collection, a pleasure due to the gracious collaboration of Her Majesty the Queen.
>
> This is, in effect, the private collection of her great-grandmother Queen Alexandra, to which have been added other pieces belonging to Her Late Majesty Queen Mary, some pieces lent by Her Majesty Queen Elizabeth the Queen Mother, and a few more from various sources. Not all the Sandringham collection is here, but the cream of it is on view; and the public has the opportunity of admiring it for the first time, for it has not been shown before.

This exhibition also marked the publication of my first book on the subject, *The Art of Carl Fabergé*. In this connection I have reason never to forget the occasion when, in 1950, as a result of my formal request, I visited Marlborough House in order to discuss with Queen Mary, the Queen Mother, the objects that had been chosen for inclusion in the book.

When I arrived I was shown by Lord Carisbrooke into a study, and when Her Majesty entered shortly afterward, she was bearing a small tray upon which rested a single gold-mounted rhodonite Easter egg about four and a half inches in height—so much for *objects,* I thought to myself! It was possible that the Queen, having dealt with the problem quite adequately for Mr. Bainbridge and his book, understandably felt that enough was enough.

There was more to come, however. Upon examination I discovered that the egg was not by the Master. Summoning what courage I could and swallowing hard, I told this imposing old lady that, beautiful though it was, this Russian egg was not by Fabergé and that to include it in a book devoted to this craftsman would be inappropriate. "Well, your father sold it to me!" came the reply. Lord Carisbrooke meantime had dragged out an enormous inventory recording Her Majesty's acquisitions. The entry was soon found and the correct description on the invoice made it quite clear that it was the work of another excellent maker, Friedrich Köchli.

The Queen was delighted—and so, needless to say, was I—and characteristically she let me have a number of her most splendid objects to include in my book.

The question of security is never far away where Fabergé is involved, and it is interesting to compare the conditions prevailing at different times. The exhibition at the Victoria and Albert Museum in London in 1977 to mark the Silver Jubilee of the Queen's reign was a comparatively simple local affair carried out with great care by the security men, but without too much fuss. The 1983 show at the Cooper-Hewitt Museum in New York, however, very properly called for far more dramatic measures—motorized police escorts, radio signals, blaring sirens, and a vast airplane called a Flying Tiger, the nose of which unexpectedly opens vertically so that the contents may be disgorged.

I marvel at our *sang-froid* when I think back to our trip up to Norfolk in 1953 to choose and gather the Royal Collection for our Coronation exhibition. My wife drove her aging Rover motor car out of the gates of Sandringham House with the objects packed in two suitcases snugly ensconced in the back under my old raincoat. Admittedly we did lock the car, but it is true to say that things really have altered quite a bit since those days.

This emphasis upon security, essential in our day, contrasts unhappily with the informality of the Edwardian era. Carl Fabergé, for his part, intended his creations to be the accoutrements of a gentler and more stylish way of life.

Alexander Schaffer in his first shop in Rockefeller Center, about 1934.

A La Vieille Russie's Fabergé

Paul Schaffer

My first awareness of Fabergé came one evening, when, during the course of recovering from the mumps or some similar childhood illness, my father brought to my bedside a lemon the size of a grapefruit. Whence came this impressive gift, destined to be transformed into two lemon meringue pies in ensuing days, and how did it end up in Long Island on our table? The answer included a brief history of Fabergé, our firm, and coincidentally something about Lillian Thomas Pratt of Fredericksburg, Virginia, whose citrus groves produced such an overwhelming souvenir. Now, having been asked to write a history of A La Vieille Russie some forty years later, I realize from that childhood memory how intertwined the story of our firm is with that of family and clients.

As I learned from my father, the Huguenot Fabergé family originated in France and moved on to Germany and then to Russia, seeking freedom to practice their religion. So, too, has the history of A La Vieille Russie been affected by religious persecution and political change. Our firm, a family affair since its founding in 1851 in Kiev, left the turmoil of the Revolution and was reestablished around 1921 in Paris by Jacques Zolotnitzky and his nephew, Léon Grinberg. They helped organize major exhibitions of Russian art in Brussels in 1928 and 1931 and in London in 1935. A La Vieille Russie, with premises on fashionable Faubourg St. Honoré, became an intellectual and trading center for the large Russian colony of the town, earned an international reputation, and was appointed jeweler to the courts of Sweden and Egypt.

Meanwhile, Alexander Schaffer, a former professional soccer player, fled the Hungarian dictatorship of Bela Kun, arriving in Paris around 1923. He settled in New York a few years later, after having spent most of his time shuttling between Russia and Western Europe, trading in merchandise acquired, in large part, in the Soviet Union. Coming to America, he worked for a time with the Hammer Galleries. Then in 1933, he and his wife, Ray, established his first retail shop, the Schaffer Collection of Russian Imperial Treasures. His trips to Russia became more frequent, bringing him often to Paris as well, where the association with members of the Zolotnitzky family deepened. With the outbreak of World War II in Europe, and with the occupation of France imminent, Schaffer provided the affidavits of support necessary for the Zolotnitzkys' immigration to the United States, which resulted in the opening in 1941 of A La Vieille Russie on New York's Fifth Avenue, first at 785, then at 781, its present location.

What the young dealer acquired during his trips to the Soviet Union were items of a general nature and not limited to Russian works of art, although these predominated. They included a great deal of porcelain, icons, brocades, and memorabilia, but relatively few items in precious materials, such as Fabergé, gold boxes, and antique jewelry, the area of his main interest. He did not travel to Russia as a collector, as did Ambassador Joseph E. Davies and his wife, Marjorie Merriweather Post, but as a dealer and trader. With $800 of borrowed capital and with his limited means he had to choose carefully; he could hardly do otherwise. Furthermore, the difficulty of traveling by boat, train, and planes of limited range—a New York to Moscow trip took several weeks—dictated a businesslike attitude, which matched the needs of the young Soviet government.

The pre-World War II period in the Soviet Union was difficult and confused, with the economy in shambles, starvation widespread, and the state in organizational and economic ruin, quite different from the political monolith and industrial power we know today. The need for hard currency was paramount, and sales of works of art were effected by various governmental agencies responsible to inexperienced ministries, who paid less attention to conserving their heritage than to raising cash by selling the confiscated property of the aristocracy and the Church to Western buyers. Whatever the collateral reasons for selling—it has been suggested that the government was proselytizing their cause while at the same time mocking the capitalists to whom they were selling—the officials involved earnestly attempted to carry out their tasks as part of the rebuilding of the country. The result was a relatively steady supply of merchandise acquired in businesslike fashion, together with tragicomic overtones.

Despite the fact that antique Russian brocades were being burned to recover their precious-metal content, or that irreplaceable eighteenth-century French silver and gold was occasionally sold for its intrinsic value, other aspects of the Soviet government's dealings were more sensible. Negotiations were often protracted and psychological, but when a bargain was struck, the deal was honored, and the goods were always sent as agreed. Once credit had been established, usually only a small deposit was required, and the merchandise was delivered then and there or shipped, with payment completed later. One example of this combination of tough bargaining and honor, at once extreme and typical, occurred during one of Alexander Schaffer's later trips. After the selection of items to be purchased, there developed a significant disagreement as to price, and finally Alex realized that a deal was impossible and requested the return of his passport so he could return home. After days of waiting in his hotel room and being told that he could not depart without agreeing to the government's terms, he was suddenly told to leave for the airport, where his passport would be returned to him. On arrival, he was surprised to find not only his passport, but also his parcel of goods, given to him as he was running to catch his plane. His offer of a receipt was refused as being unnecessary. Needless to say, he got the goods at his price.

So much for the flavor of his trips to the Soviet Union. Although Fabergé was only a small part of what Schaffer was able to purchase during his first trips, his fascination with the technical skill of the artists related to his interest in eighteenth-century French gold boxes, and he began to buy more and more. For the most part, Fabergé had a practical commercial advantage in addition to its artistic appeal—it was relatively reasonable in price. Since the pieces were almost new, he was able to buy quite a number of items for a modest sum; he could have a whole garden of Fabergé flowers or a menagerie of animals to choose from and be able to sell them for $300 to $400 each. The silver was purchased by weight, and that too could be offered at affordable prices. Items like cane handles, frames, clocks, and other smaller pieces including the miniature eggs likewise sold for less than $50 apiece. (Miniature eggs by Fabergé and those by other Russian jewelers cost about the same, priced according to their quality rather than their authorship as is done today.)

On display in the shop in the 1930s were many other modestly priced items such as a seventeenth-century icon for $12, Gardner plates of the Order of St. Vladimir at $35 each, and a dozen cloisonné enamel spoons for $60, to mention only a few. Porcelain eggs with the monogram of Alexandra Feodorovna, now selling for several hundred dollars, were boxed and offered as gifts to favored clients at Easter time, as were Fabergé's wartime brass and copper ashtrays. In short, there was a large variety of merchandise to choose from, and the imperial origins of many of the pieces bearing labels from imperial palaces and aristocratic estates added to their interest.

Most desirable, then as now, were the Fabergé items, whose extraordinary detail and exquisite charm gained the gallery many clients, including Lillian Thomas Pratt, Marjorie Merriweather Post, and India E. Minshall, whose Fabergé collections form the nuclei of the Russian collections at the Virginia Museum of Fine Arts, Hillwood, and the Cleveland Museum of Art. In 1936, when The Schaffer Collection, including much Fabergé, was exhibited to celebrate the move to larger quarters at 15 West 50th Street, the increased demand for Fabergé was such that a presentation box then commanded as much as $2,500 and an Imperial Egg over $10,000, which, by Depression standards, were strong prices indeed. As the gallery's clientele grew, and as the Schaffers' fascination with Fabergé increased, buying trips became more frequent and included longer stays in Western Europe, where the Russian aristocracy had fled with many valuable possessions, although the majority of the stock was still acquired in Russia.

Records of this prewar period are sketchy, but it is of interest to note a few transactions, which are cited merely as representative of the period. Furthermore, an attempt at exactitude is complicated by the fact that many descriptions are brief, making positive identification of pieces known today the exception. This is not surprising: given the modest cost of many pieces, elaborate descriptions were not warranted. A gold and enamel clock, for instance, cost $65, a gold and enamel frame $95, a buckle $15, and a stone animal $135. There were a few exceptions: the circular blue enamel presentation box with the monogram of Nicholas II (exhibited A La Vieille Russie 1983, no. 218) had been purchased in 1923 for $250, sold in 1930 for about $700, and resold in 1979 for $42,800; the twelve-panel pink enamel Easter egg now in the collection of Her Majesty the Queen was sold in 1933 for about $850; the Coronation Box now owned by the FORBES Magazine Collection was sold in 1937 for about $1,700, with a profit of about $350; the rich *mujik* (exhibited Victoria and Albert Museum 1977, no. N5) was sold in 1937 for $950, with a $200 profit; and a red enamel cigarette case (exhibited A La Vieille Russie 1983, no. 118) was purchased in the mid-1930s for $54 and sold in 1975 for about $8,000. Also illustrative are the deals that were not made: the smoky topaz vase (exhibited A La Vieille Russie 1983, no. 309) was turned down in 1938 when offered for $1,350, and the cloisonné enamel tea set (H. C. Bainbridge, plate no. 36) was turned down in 1940 when offered by Fabergé's son in Paris for $1,500. Although the prices seem low today, they were only relatively so; if proof is needed, one can observe that, as a Fabergé lorgnette in its original case was priced at $67.50, a dollar was indeed worth halving! The firm, after all, had its formative years during the Great Depression.

But the history of a firm is told only in part by the merchandise it deals in; A La Vieille Russie was also shaped by its clients, who, after all, are the raison d'être of any business and, more important, have the courage to act on their instincts, becoming the tastemakers of their generation. Furthermore, during the early years of our business, starting as it did with limited capital at the bottom of a depression and with largely unknown merchandise, the relationship between client and dealer was exceptionally close as together they explored virgin territory. Particularly important in this equation was Alex's wife, Ray, who did not accompany him on his early buying trips but worked closely with clients in forming their collections.

It was in this period that the Peter the Great Egg came on the market and was offered to numerous dealers here and abroad, most of whom branded Schaffer insane for handling such a "modern" piece. But it was always his opinion that it was the most important

Alexander Schaffer with Mrs. Maurice Utrillo and Armand Hammer at the opening of the Utrillo exhibition organized jointly by A La Vieille Russie and Hammer Galleries in 1958.

piece of Fabergé he had ever sold, and the memory of the scornful adjective as uttered by an English friend—"modun"—remained with him the rest of his life. Mrs. Pratt, of course, fell in love with it and added it to her collection. As with most of the important pieces of Fabergé, it was expensive and beyond the reach of the average buyer, but being a true collector, she stretched her purse a little and paid for it in monthly installments. What a pleasure to have been able to exhibit this marvel of craftsmanship and historical commemoration recently, and to once again hold it in our hands. It is now universally recognized as a masterpiece, with no one doubting its value.

The war years brought numerous changes. During this period, however, interest in Fabergé remained, and Schaffer managed to buy pieces from important collections, operating the business more or less as usual.

After the war, travel to the Soviet Union resumed, although trips were not as frequent or as successful, nor were they easily organized. An invitation had to be received from the Soviet government, permission from the United States Passport Agency had to be requested, stating the purpose of the visit and asking if there were any objections, and finally, the Allied High Command had to be petitioned to travel through Poland and Austria in order to reach Russia. But if these postwar trips to Russia were less successful, Europe still had much to offer, and in 1949 our first postwar exhibition of Fabergé was held, with 291 pieces on view, in conjunction with the publication of H. C. Bainbridge's *Peter Carl Fabergé*. By 1954, when King Farouk's collection, which we had helped form, was dispersed—an adventure in itself—the world was recovering. New collectors had entered the market, and prices had begun to advance significantly from the relatively steady period of the 1930s and 1940s.

Chief among these collectors were Mr. and Mrs. Jack Linsky and Mr. and Mrs. Lansdell K. Christie. The Linskys' Fabergé was denigrated by James Rorimer, then director of The Metropolitan Museum of Art, and their collection was sold. Once interest in Fabergé had risen again, and The Metropolitan had a new director, the museum reversed its policy and displayed the Lansdell K. Christie Collection on semi-permanent loan in an especially designed gallery. Unfortunately, Christie died before he could make plans for a permanent installation at the Metropolitan, and once again the museum lost an opportunity to obtain some Fabergé treasures. The sale of Christie's Fabergé was handled by A La Vieille Russie (most of his collection was exhibited anonymously in our second major postwar Fabergé exhibition in 1961). Many of the important pieces, including the Imperial Eggs, were purchased by the FORBES Magazine Collection, now the largest in the world.

In all, we've handled about half of the important Easter eggs, at least a dozen figurines, and thousands of other pieces by Fabergé, and in the fifty years we have been in New York, we've gone from a time when ours was the task of educating the public—showing, teaching, and explaining—to a time when our task is simply finding new things, although now without Alex. In 1972, on his way to the sale of a collection of snuffboxes partially formed by us and owned by the late Charles Engelhard, Alex died in Paris, the city of his youth. The business is being carried on by Ray Schaffer and the two sons, Paul and Peter. Grandchildren next? Who knows!

Perhaps one of our more successful window displays illustrates the interest and knowledge of an increasing number of collectors. In this display, stacks of pre-Revolutionary currency, now valueless, were shown next to fine works of art by Fabergé. Passersby nodded knowingly, realizing that a beautiful object created by man is more lasting than either man or his folly. Proof of the universal appeal of these precious objects came again recently in 1983 during our third postwar exhibition of Fabergé works, the largest and most successful, when thousands queued up patiently to see it.

We are inspired by the thought, reinforced by the reception of this exhibition, that we at A La Vieille Russie have executed our duties of conservatorship and education well and faithfully, and hope to continue into our second century of operation with the help of farseeing and imaginative clients—our good friends and best students.

Group of Fabergé Boxes. Clockwise from left: Love Trophy Bonbonnière by Perchin, made of gold, blue, and white enamel, crystal, and diamonds. Vial with Rose Trellis Lid, by Wigström, made of rock crystal, gold, pink, and green enamel, and diamonds. Box with Views of the Fortress of St. Peter and St. Paul by Wigström, made of gold, oyster-rose, white, green, and sepia enamel, diamonds, and pearls. Vinaigrette, made of gold, turquoise blue and dark green enamel, and diamonds.

The King of Siam visiting Czar Nicholas II at Tsarko Selo in 1897. Seated, left to right: Grand Duchess Olga, King Chulalongkorn, Dowager Empress Marie Feodorovna, the Czar, and Crown Prince Vajiravudh. Standing are other members of the entourage.

Fabergé in Thailand

Roy D. R. Betteley

Oval brooch in gold and enamel, framed with a narrow band of calibre-cut rubies interrupted by four rose-cut diamonds and edged with a border of diamonds in a flamelike Thai design; contains a miniature of three royal Siamese children. Height, 1 inch. Made by Holmström.

In November 1981, Her Majesty Queen Sirikit of Thailand visited Hillwood, the home of the late Marjorie Merriweather Post in Washington, D. C., which is now open to the public as a museum. The Queen knew of the Russian and French decorative art on display at Hillwood and expressed special interest in seeing the Fabergé objects in the collection. In the course of her tour, the Queen, who was wearing a brooch by Fabergé containing a miniature portrait of a member of the Thai royal family, mentioned the Thai Royal Fabergé Collection in Bangkok and told us that a member of the royal family had gone to Russia as a student during the reign of Czar Nicholas II.

Nearly two years after this visit, Mrs. Yoopa Pranich, a Washington resident and personal friend of Her Majesty the Queen, came to Hillwood. The Thai Royal Fabergé Collection was discussed and it was suggested that representatives from Hillwood might go to Bangkok to examine it. With the Queen's consent, arrangements for the visit were made.

The Hillwood team that went with me consisted of Sally B. Lilley, a former Hillwood guide who joined us from Taiwan, Jeannette M. Harper, a longtime Hillwood guide who had shown Mrs. Pranich the collections, and my wife, Paulette, who is experienced in the identification of gems and hardstones. The group assembled in Bangkok in late June 1983.

It might be interesting to provide some historical background concerning the period when Fabergé objects were acquired by the Thai royal family nearly one hundred years ago, most of them during the reign of His Majesty King Chulalongkorn (1868-1910).

Cane handle in the form of a rabbit's head in rock crystal with ruby eyes; collar in ruby-red enamel edged in silver, on a shaft of wood. Length, 11⅝ inches.

The major contact between the Romanovs of Russia and the Chakri dynasty of Siam during the era of the Fabergé workshops was the visit to St. Petersburg made by His Majesty King Chulalongkorn in 1897. At least one Fabergé object was presented to the King by Czar Nicholas II on that occasion.

Actually, the first meeting between these two men had taken place seven years earlier when Nicholas, then the Czarevitch, sailed on a naval cruise aboard the *Pamyat Azova*. He stopped in Siam in March 1890, where he was the guest of King Chulalongkorn. Upon his departure, the King gave Nicholas two elephants and a white monkey to take back to Russia as presents for his father, Czar Alexander III. One elephant died on the homeward voyage, but the other two animals survived and it is said that the Czar liked the monkey very much. Later that same year, in gratitude for his hospitality to the Czarevitch, Alexander bestowed the Order of St. Andrew, the highest order of Russia, on King Chulalongkorn.

In 1897 when King Chulalongkorn visited Nicholas II, his visit was probably political, its main purpose being to seek the Czar's intercession with France concerning her aggressive adventures into Siam, which threatened its political and territorial integrity. The King arrived in St. Petersburg on July 3, 1897, and two days later informed his Minister of Foreign Affairs in Bangkok that discussions had taken place regarding problems involving Siam and France, and that the Russians had agreed that the Czar would approach the French government on the matter.

Whatever the original purpose of the 1897 visit, it resulted in a long and continuing contact between the two royal families and the important establishment of official diplomatic ties between the two countries.

King Chulalongkorn had been accompanied by his fifteen-year-old son, His Royal Highness Prince Chakrabongse, who remained in Russia as a student after his father returned to Siam. Prince Chakrabongse attended the Corps des Pages and was treated as a member of the Czar's family. During this time, many of the Fabergé objects now in the Thai Royal Collection were undoubtedly sent to the Siamese royal family as gifts from the Czar, and perhaps from the Prince himself, and there were also commissions to the Fabergé workshops from the Siamese monarch.

Prince Chakrabongse rose to the rank of captain in the Hussars, and in 1906 married an eighteen-year-old Russian woman, Catherine Denitski, who had served as a nurse in the Russo-Japanese War of 1905. Their granddaughter married an Englishman and is believed to be living in Cornwall today.

But now to return to our arrival at the Grand Palace in Bangkok on June 19, 1983. We found that Her Majesty the Queen had arranged for the Fabergé pieces to be assembled and displayed in a large state

The Tenniel illustration for Lewis Carroll's *Through the Looking Glass* that inspired the Fabergé figurines.

Below: Pair of hardstone figurines representing Tweedledum and Tweedledee, with face and hands in jasper, diamond eyes, hats and socks in lapis lazuli, jackets in purpurine with gold buttons, boots in black jasper, and breeches in bowenite.

Small box by Wigström, made of nephrite, gold, and diamonds, with opalescent sepia enamel view of The Temple of Dawn.

Below right: Frame by Nevalainen of silver gilt, yellow-green enamel, silver, mounted on mahogany plaque. Contains photograph of King Chulalongkorn.

chamber, alongside outstanding examples of the work of Thai artisans. It was a most impressive display.

Our procedure for examining the Fabergé pieces was to identify the marks, describe the piece, measure it, and photograph it. In this process we handled 72 pieces, the majority of which bore workmasters' initials; among them Henrik Wigström's were prominent. In several instances we were able to photograph pieces in their original Fabergé boxes. Age and climate had caused several of the boxes to disintegrate, and they required patching before they could be photographed.

The Fabergé pieces in the Thai Royal Collection can be divided into two groups. One group consists of pieces that are the personal property of the King, and which can be disposed of as he sees fit. The other group consists of pieces that are the property of the Crown, and which must be passed on to the King's successor. The pieces in this second category, which have been used for official ceremonies or have religious significance, are all made of nephrite and include a large shallow round bowl supported by three figures, two small shallow round bowls, two matching three-branched candelabra, one large deep bowl, a round box, and a large kovsh.

The large nephrite bowl supported by three figures in gold has been used to hold holy water for administering the oath of allegiance to high court officials, a ceremony which takes place in the Chapel of the Emerald Buddha. We were told that the gold used in the making of the three supporting figures was personally supplied by King Chulalongkorn. The workmanship of these three figures is extraordinary. It was the only Fabergé piece for which we recorded the weight as well as the dimensions: it weighed over twenty pounds! Henry Bainbridge, in *Peter Carl Fabergé*, refers to the figures' being made of gold. Kenneth Snowman, in *Carl Fabergé*, also writes of the large nephrite bowl supported by three figures—but he describes them as being made of silver gilt. We can report that the feet upon which the piece rests are indeed silver gilt.

The collection also contains three other significant items in nephrite: the large Buddha, which is kept in the King's Private Chapel in the Grand Palace; the small Buddha, which is kept in the Royal Family Chapel in Chitralada Palace; and the bell and small round box in which Her Majesty keeps relics of Buddha.

The existence of these large nephrite pieces has been known for many years. Bainbridge mentions an "Image of Buddha" kept in the Temple of the Emerald Buddha "and throughout the reign of King Rama VI used in various official ceremonies"; he also cites a shallow bowl, a pair of candlesticks, and another image of Buddha, housed in Thailand's National Museum. Bainbridge includes photographs, furnished by the Siamese government, of the small Buddha, the large shallow bowl, and the large nephrite bowl, but he omits details of

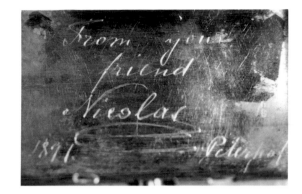

Engraved in gold on a Fabergé gift to King Chulalongkorn a year after their meeting: "From your friend Nicolas."

Large Buddha in nephrite, 15 inches high, in attitude of dispelling evil. The base is inscribed "Fabergé 1914." This is kept in the King's Private Chapel.

Penknife by Wigström, made of gold, engraved with floral bouquets and enameled apple green. Used by ladies of the court to peel and cut fresh fruit.

Cigarette Case by Wigström, made of three-color gold, white enamel, diamonds. Contains cigarette holder of jasper, white enamel, and gold.

Detail of gold support for large nephrite bowl. Mythical Brahmin figure of The Garuda, made of gold, diamonds, rubies, and emeralds, resting on nephrite base with feet in silver gilt.

their size because this information had not been included with the photographs.

Bainbridge also addressed the matter of Fabergé's visit to Siam, reporting that "the invitation to visit Siam came from King Chulalongkorn . . . in 1904," and adding that "Fabergé was especially fortunate in going to Siam just in time when there was a call not only for objects of fantasy but for much jewelry and not only for the Royal House but for Siamese aristocracy." We understand that a member of Fabergé's family did, in fact, go to Bangkok in November, 1908.

During World War II Prime Minister Pibul Songgram sent most of the precious objects to Petchabun for safekeeping. Later they were returned to the Grand Palace in Bangkok, but until about 1982 most of the objects had remained packed.

It is not possible in the space available here to include pictures of all the pieces we saw and photographed, but we have made a representative selection.

Our visit to the Grand Palace was an exceptional experience for each of us. We felt especially privileged and honored to have seen the Thai Royal Fabergé Collection, which had never been shown to the public and never before in its entirety to anyone. During our stay we were especially impressed by the kindness, cooperation, and hospitality invariably shown us by the palace staff and by the Thai people from all walks of life with whom we came in contact. This, of course, contributed immensely to making our visit such a pleasant and memorable event.

Above: Oval Kovsh by Wigström, made of nephrite, gold, rose diamonds, strawberry red enamel.

Left: Bell and stand by Wigström, made of nephrite, red jade, red gold, white enamel, diamonds, moonstones, and white pearl.

Opposite: The Princess Marina of Kent Pansy, by Wigström, made of enameled gold and hardstone with rose-cut diamonds, nephrite, and rock crystal.

Chronology of the House of Fabergé

The Fabergé family, of French Huguenot origin, left France in 1685. After living for several generations in Germany they settled in what was then the Russian Baltics, at Pernau in Estonia. Here Gustav Fabergé is born in 1814.

1842   Gustav Fabergé starts a jewelry business in Bolshaya Morskaya Street, St. Petersburg.

1846   Carl Fabergé born in St. Petersburg on May 30, son of Gustav Fabergé and his wife Charlotte, née Jungstedt. He is baptized in the Protestant church with the name Peter Carl, but in Russian is called Karl Gustavovich.

1870   Carl Fabergé takes over his father's firm. After finishing school he is apprenticed to Hiskias Pendin, workmaster with Gustav Fabergé. On qualifying as journeyman he makes trips to Germany, Switzerland, and France, to study art and economics.

1872   Fabergé marries Augusta Julia Jacobs. They have four sons: Eugène (1874-1960), Agathon (1876-1951), Alexander (1877-1952), and Nicholas (1884-1939), all of whom eventually join the firm.

1881   Death of Czar Alexander II.

1882   Fabergé's younger brother, twenty-year-old Agathon, returns from Dresden to join the firm. For the first time the House of Fabergé exhibits at the Pan-Russian Exhibition in Moscow and wins a Gold Medal. The shop moves to 16 Bolshaya Morskaya Street.

1885   First Imperial Easter Egg made for Empress Marie Feodorovna at the request of Alexander III, who grants his Imperial Warrant to the firm.
   Gold medal at the Nuremberg Exhibition of Applied Arts for replicas of the Scythian Treasure, made by workmaster Erik Kollin. The catalogue identifies Fabergé as being "Jeweller of His Majesty and of the Imperial Hermitage."

1886   Michael Perchin joins House of Fabergé and becomes firm's head workmaster.

1887   Moscow branch opens. Allan Bowe becomes partner.

1888   Special diploma awarded at the Nordic Exhibition, Copenhagen, where Fabergé exhibits *hors concours*.

1890   St. Petersburg premises doubles in size. Branch opens in Odessa.

1893   Death of Gustav Fabergé in Dresden.

1894   Death of Alexander III. The new Czar, Nicholas II, marries Princess Alix of Hesse-Darmstadt, who becomes the Empress Alexandra Feodorovna. Eugène Fabergé joins firm.

1895   Death of Fabergé's brother Agathon.

1896   Coronation of Nicholas II. House of Fabergé awarded State Emblem at the Pan-Russian Exhibition, Nijny-Novgorod.

1897   Nordic Exhibition, Stockholm. Fabergé exhibits *hors concours,* as Eugène Fabergé is a member of the jury. Royal Warrant of the Court of Sweden and Norway granted.

1898   Premises bought at 24 Bolshaya Morskaya Street for a million rubles. Reconstruction started under direction of architect Carl Schmidt, a Fabergé nephew.

1900   Removal to the new premises, which contain the shop, Fabergé's private apartment, many workshops, and several of the master goldsmiths' living quarters.
   World Exhibition in Paris: three Imperial Easter Eggs exhibited at the request of the two czarinas. Fabergé acclaimed *Maître* and decorated with Legion of Honor.

1901 Death of workmaster Erik Kollin.

1902 Exhibition of Imperial Easter Eggs in St. Petersburg in the Palace of Grand Duke Vladimir.

1903 Arthur Bowe starts Fabergé branch in London at Berners Hotel.
Death of Michael Perchin, whose workshop is taken over by Henrik Wigström. Death of August Holmström, who is succeeded by his son Albert.

1904 Fabergé invited to visit the King of Siam.

1905 Branch opens in Kiev.

1906 London branch opens shop at 48 Dover Street under direction of Nicholas Fabergé and H. C. Bainbridge.

1909 Death of Alfred Thielemann.

1910 Kiev branch closes.

1911 London branch moves to 173 New Bond Street.

1913 Tercentenary of Romanov rule.

1915 London branch officially closes. Death of August Hollming.

1916 Firm is transformed into a joint-stock company with a capital of 3,000,000 rubles and 600 shares.
Death of Julius Rappoport.

1917 Outbreak of the Russian Revolution in Petrograd. Firm is taken over by a "Committee of the Employees of the Company K. Fabergé."
London branch stock is acquired by the jewelers Lacloche Frères of Paris.

1918 Carl Fabergé escapes with the aid of the British Embassy. House of Fabergé finally closed down.

1920 Fabergé arrives in Lausanne in June and dies there on September 24.

1929 Fabergé's ashes buried at Cannes by his eldest son, Eugène.

LAST ECHOES OF THE FABERGÉ NAME

In the early 1920s, Carl Fabergé's sons Eugène and Alexander settled in Paris. Around 1924, with Andrea Marchetti and Guerrieri they opened a firm under the name "Fabergé & Cie, Paris." There they produced objects in the style of the original House, but with only moderate success. The firm still exists in Paris but no longer has any direct connection with the Fabergé family. Eugène Fabergé died in Paris in 1953.

During the 1930s, in the United States, Sam Rubin began producing perfumes under the name "Fabergé." Between 1945 and 1951 the Paris firm started litigation against Rubin for using the name, which, however, had never been registered or copyrighted. In 1951 an agreement was reached by which Rubin paid the Paris firm $25,000 for the right to use the name for toiletries and perfumes only.

Alexander Fabergé was later recorded as having a workshop in Finland. Two grandsons of Carl Fabergé, Theo and Igor, worked as jewelry designers in Geneva. Igor Fabergé died in 1982.

A. v. S.

Workshops and Workmasters

The firm of the Russian goldsmith and jeweler Fabergé is one of the best in the world. In its branches in Petersburg and Moscow more than 500 artists and craftsmen work. The firm has been in existence for seventy years and in that time has produced a vast quantity of *objets d'art* which are scattered all over the world. Aside from being purveyor to His Majesty and nearly all the foreign courts, Fabergé works on commission for American millionaires and wealthy English people; he is now finishing a commission for the King of Siam.

This introduction from a Russian article published in St. Petersburg in *Stolitsa i Usadba* in 1914 gives an impression of the size and scope of the House of Fabergé. In fact, the workshops with 500 employees had to be well organized to produce *objets d'art* of the high quality for which the firm was famous. This production was masterminded by Carl Fabergé; it can be said that he himself was more an entrepreneur and manager than an artist. Consequently he only assigned the original idea for the creation of an object, which was then worked out by the individual artists or workmasters. In the last analysis, he was essentially a supervisor of the production which was—in spite of the large quantity of objects—always of supreme technical perfection. The workmasters, who had the right to sign their objects, were themselves interested in maintaining the high standard of quality. They were never treated by Fabergé simply as anonymous employees but were respected as individual artists.

H. C. Bainbridge, Fabergé's representative in London, describes the premises and workshops in St. Petersburg in *Twice Seven:*

When Fabergé moved into the great Gothic building in the Bolshaya Morskaya he had the advantage of having everything under one roof. As well as the shop, which was more like a large reception hall, and his private apartments on a higher floor, the studios and main workshops were all arranged so that everything was under his immediate control and that of his seconds-in-command, his sons Eugène and Agathon. Each workmaster was an Artist Craftsman who rented his workshop from Fabergé and em-

ployed his own workmen. I remember Wigstroem well, a big jolly man who made the *fantaisie* articles enamelled on gold and silver such as cigarette cases, umbrella tops and bonbonnières and also the Easter eggs for the Imperial Family. The precious metals and stones were supplied to him by the firm, as well as the finished designs to which he had to work. When an article was finished, and often when it was in an unfinished state, it was brought down to Fabergé for examination and criticism, and when passed was paid for. By this arrangement the workmaster was relieved of the heavy expenses of materials and had constant work. He was paid regularly and Fabergé was in immediate touch with each article in the process of its making.

A letter, now in the Shrewsbury Museum, England, from Allan Bowe, director of Fabergé's Moscow branch, to J. Oswald Jones, an Englishman who was to be employed as a jewelry designer, describes the working conditions in Moscow. It can be presumed that the conditions at the St. Petersburg workshop were similar.

17/30 December, 1901

Your letter of the 21st inst & two parcels of designs & sketches have arrived. To judge by both the letter & the sketches, I think that you would suit us. At first you will find a certain difficulty in working to order, that is, making designs to meet the many requirements of customers. I also notice that you show me no jewelry work, where diamonds & other stones are used. This will have to be learnt. However, as you are young, you will, after 6 months' work (if you go at it seriously) find yourself a full-fledged jeweler's artist—& that is what I want.

Now to business. I offer you 160 rubles a month salary—which makes exactly £17—The hours of work are: Winter, from 9 till 7, with one interval of an hour for lunch. Summer, from 10 till 6, with one hour for lunch. These are the hours of my establishment & no exception can be made.

You would work in a large, light & warm room above the shop, where all my designers are. You are under nobody but myself—so that there is no possibility of being bullied by any overseer &c.

You would work only for the jewelry department—silver having its own men.

Living: I have made enquiries, & find that you can be boarded & lodged in a decent & comfortable way, in an English family, for 60 rubles (£6-8) a month, which would leave you 110 rubles a month to spend. We have a colony of about 300-350 English men and Women in Moscow, & among them you are sure to make some friends. I have four Englishmen (more or less so) in the shop.

In Moscow the objects were signed only with the name "K. Fabergé" in Cyrillic letters together with the double-headed eagle as emblem of the Imperial Warrant. But in St. Petersburg, the individual workmaster had the right to sign his objects with a mark showing his

Opposite: Design for a pendant with imperial eagle; gouache, from the Fabergé workshop in Petrograd between 1914 and 1917. Signed K. Fabergé.

initials next to the mark of the firm. Collectors were long puzzled by the absence of the Imperial eagle on St. Petersburg pieces and its unvarying presence on Moscow work, where the Fabergé signature appears with the initial K. The reason for this lies in the fact that the Imperial Warrant was held personally by Carl Fabergé for his firm, and not by the workmasters.

There are, however, three exceptions to this rule: pieces bearing the signatures of Nevalainen, Rappoport, or Wäkevä may also, although made in St. Petersburg, have the double-headed eagle as individual punch next to the Fabergé signature. These three men were among the senior workmasters and actually had independent workshops. They apparently had received the Imperial Warrant in their own rights.

The following is a list of all workmasters known to have worked for Fabergé who had the right to sign their objects with their initials.

Karl Gustav Hjalmar Armfeldt.

Johan VICTOR AARNE (1863-1934), born in Finland; Fabergé workmaster from 1891 to 1904. After selling his workshop to Hjalmar Armfeldt in 1904, he opened his own workshop in Viipuri, Finland. His signature is to be found on gold and silver articles, often enameled.

FEDOR AFANASSIEV made small articles of high quality in enamel: miniature Easter eggs, small frames, and cigarette cases.

Karl Gustav HJALMAR ARMFELDT (1873-1959), born in Finland, workmaster under Anders Nevalainen from 1895 until 1904. Studied at the German art school at St. Petersburg 1887-89 and at Baron Stieglitz's school for applied arts 1889-1904. In 1904 he bought the workshop of Victor Aarne and became workmaster for Fabergé on the recommendation of Aarne and Nevalainen. He mainly produced enameled objects for Fabergé until 1916. Armfeldt emigrated to Finland, where he worked from 1920 on.

ANDREJ GORIANOV took over from Reimer after his death in 1898. He specialized in small gold and enamel objects and cigarette cases.

AUGUST Fredrik HOLLMING (1854-1913), born in Finland, workmaster in St. Petersburg from 1880 until his death, with a workshop at 35 Kazanskaya Street; in 1900 he moved into Fabergé's new building. For Fabergé he produced gold and silver boxes and ornaments, some of them enameled. Occasionally he made small enameled jewelry. Mark:

His son, August Väinö Hollming (1885-1934), ran his father's workshop from 1913 until 1918.

AUGUST Wilhelm HOLMSTRÖM (1829-1903), born in Helsinki, workmaster in 1857 with his own workshop. Senior member of Fabergé's firm; he was head jeweler and is recorded as the maker of the 1892 Diamond Trellis Egg. Mark: A.H.

His son, ALBERT Woldemar HOLMSTRÖM (1876-1925), took over the workshop at his father's death in 1903 and continued to work in St. Petersburg until 1918; later in Finland.

One daughter, Hilma Alina, worked as a jewelry designer for Fabergé. Another daughter, Fanny Florentina, married workmaster Knut Oskar Pihl.

ERIK August KOLLIN (1836-1901), born in Finland, qualified as workmaster in 1868; in 1870 opened his own workshop in St. Petersburg at 9 Kazanskaya Street. Kollin worked exclusively for Fabergé, and was soon put in charge of all Fabergé workshops, a post he held until 1886 when he was replaced by Michael Perchin. He specialized in gold and silver articles. The replicas of the Scythian Treasures, exhibited at the 1885 Nuremberg Exhibition, were made in his workshop.

Karl GUSTAV Johansson LUNDELL (1833-?) is not recorded as qualified master, but worked for Fabergé's Odessa branch.

ANDERS MICHELSSON (1839-1913), born in Finland, was master goldsmith and jeweler by 1867. He mainly produced gold cigarette cases and small enameled objects.

August Hollming.

August Holmström.

Anders Nevalainen.

ANDERS Johan NEVALAINEN (1858-1933), born in Finland, became master in 1885. He worked exclusively for Fabergé, first in August Holmström's workshop, then independently in his own. He made small articles in gold and silver, including enameled frames and cigarette cases.

GABRIEL Zachariasson NIUKKANEN, master between 1898 and 1912 with his own workshop in St. Petersburg at 39 Kazanskaya Street. He made plain gold cigarette cases, which only on occasion bore Fabergé's signature.

MICHAEL Evlampievich PERCHIN (1860-1903), born in Petrozavodsk, Eastern Karelia, died in St. Petersburg. Perchin, Fabergé's legendary workmaster, was head of the workshops from 1886 until his death. His workshop was at 11 Bolshaya Morskaya Street until 1900 when he moved to Fabergé's new premises at number 24. His workshop produced all types of *objets de fantaisie* in gold, enamel, and hardstones. He was responsible for the Imperial Easter Eggs made between 1886 and 1903.

He used two punches: one rectangular, one oval, which both appear on the 1897 Coronation Easter Egg. It may be suggested that the rectangular mark was probably used from 1886 until 1897, and the oval punch was applied from 1897 to 1903.

Knut OSKAR PIHL (1860-1897), born in Finland, workmaster in 1887, manufactured small jewelry pieces. He married a daughter of August Holmström.

Pihl's daughter, Alma Teresia Pihl (1888-1976), started as a jewelry designer in the workshop of her uncle, Albert Holmström. She made the designs of the 1913 Winter Egg and the 1914 Mosaic Egg.

JULIUS Alexandrovich RAPPOPORT (1864-1916), had his own workshop at Ekatarininski Canal from 1883, where he remained when Fabergé moved his staff to the house in Bolshaya Morskaya Street. Rappoport was head silversmith and produced large objects and services, as well as silver animals.

WILHELM REIMER (died c. 1898), born in Pernau, Lettland, made small enamel and gold objects.

Philip THEODOR RINGE had his own workshop from 1893 on, where he made objects in enameled gold or silver.

FEDOR RÜCKERT, born in Moscow, of German origin, made articles in Moscow in cloisonné enamel. Fabergé's Moscow signature often obliterates Rückert's initials. Rückert also sold his cloisonné objects independently, which explains why a number of his pieces bear no Fabergé signature.

EDUARD Wilhelm SCHRAMM, born in St. Petersburg, of German origin, worked for Fabergé before 1899 making cigarette cases and gold objects; in most instances he signed only with his own initials.

VLADIMIR SOLOVIEV took over Ringe's workshop after his death, and made similar objects. His initials can often be found under the enamel on pieces made for export to England.

ALFRED THIELEMANN (date of birth unknown, died between 1890 and 1910), of German origin, master from 1858 and active as jeweler for Fabergé from 1880. Thielemann produced trinkets and small pieces of jewelry; his place was taken after his death by his son, Karl Rudolph Thielemann.

The mark AT was also used by three other masters who did not work for Fabergé: Alexander Tillander produced objects in the style of Fabergé for the firm of Hahn; A. Tobinkov was a workmaster in the firm of silversmiths Nichols & Plincke; the third was A. Treiden.

STEFAN WÄKEVÄ (1833-1910), born in Finland, master in 1856. He made silver articles for practical use.

His son, ALEXANDER WÄKEVÄ (1870-1957), was trained as a silver-smith with his father and took over the workshop in 1910.

HENRIK Immanuel WIGSTRÖM (1862-1923), born in Taminisaari, Finland. In 1884 he obtained a post as journeyman with Michael Perchin. After Perchin's death in 1903, Wigström became head workmaster of Fabergé until 1917. Under his direction, the Imperial Easter Eggs were made from 1904 to 1917. Nearly all hardstone animals, figurines, and flowers were produced under his super-vision.

His son, Henrik Wilhelm Wigström (1889-1934), was apprenticed to his fa-ther and worked with him until 1917.

The First Silver *Artel,* a cooperative of in-dependent jewelers, goldsmiths, and sil-versmiths, worked for Fabergé between 1890 and 1917, producing silver articles including animals and a number of ob-jects in guilloché enamel.

There are other unidentified workmas-ters' marks appearing in conjunction with Fabergé's signature

Henrik Wigström.

The painters of the miniatures that ap-pear on Fabergé objects include:

A. BLAZNOV. No biographical details known. Painted mainly portraits of Nicholas II during the 1890s. The signa-ture is usually in Cyrillic.

KONSTANTIN KRIJITSKI (Krizhitsky). Painted miniatures for the 1891 Cauca-sus Egg and for the 1895 Danish Palace Egg. The latter are on mother-of-pearl.

PRACHOV. No biographical details known. Painted the icon of the Resurrec-tion of Christ for the 1915 Red Cross Egg.

JOHANNES ZEHNGRAF. Born 1857 in Copenhagen, died 1908 in Berlin. Chief miniature painter for Fabergé. Painted portraits of the Imperial Family, the King and Queen of Denmark, King Ferdinand I of Bulgaria. Three Imperial Easter Eggs are decorated with his miniatures, including the 1898 Lilies of the Valley Egg.

VASILY ZUIEV. Active from about 1908 to 1917, possibly succeeding Zehngraf as chief miniaturist. Remained in Russia after the Revolution. A brilliant artist, he painted not only on ivory but also on enamel. Major examples of his work are the miniatures on ivory of the 1911 Fifteenth Anniversary Egg and the grisaille enamel panels of the 1914 Grisaille Egg (now called the Catherine the Great Egg).

Also recorded, but with little or no details known, are the names of de Benckendorff, I. Geftler, S. Solomko, Horace Wallick, and A. Wegner.

A. v. S.

Marks on Fabergé objects

The workshop of August Wilhelm Holmström, head jeweler of Fabergé, and his son, Albert, at the firm's premises, 24 Bolshaya Morskaya Street, St. Petersburg.

THE HALLMARKS

These marks guarantee that an item was made of precious metal. The Russian gold and silver standards were reckoned in zolotniks — 96 zolotniks correspond to 24-carat gold and to pure silver. The most frequently found proportions for silver alloys are 84 and 88 zolotniks; objects with 91-zolotnik marks were often made for export. These standards correspond to 875, 916 and 947/1000 respectively, while sterling silver is 925/1000. For gold the Russian standard marks are 56 and 72 zolotniks, corresponding to 14- and 18-carat gold.

	St. Petersburg	Moscow
Late 19th century (until 1899)	**56**	**Л.О 1894 88**
1899-1908	**56**	**84**
1908-1917	**72**	**88**

Opposite: The Fabergé shop in St. Petersburg. Georg Stein, the workmaster who made the miniature carriage for the Coronation Egg, is in the center selling a necklace to Grand Duke Cyril Vladimirovich.

The Fabergé signatures

ST. PETERSBURG Fabergé's full signature (without initials) in Cyrillic characters

ФАБЕРЖЕ

Silver objects from the workshops of Nevalainen, Rappoport, Wäkevä and the First Silver *Artel* (ICA) have the signature in Cyrillic with the initial K. and the Imperial Warrant in a separate punch

К.ФАБЕРЖЕ

Fabergé's initials in Cyrillic characters for small objects

КФ

Objects, usually made for export, can be marked with Fabergé's full name or his initials in Roman letters

FABERGE CF

MOSCOW Objects made in the Moscow workshop are marked K. Fabergé in Cyrillic characters, together with the double-headed eagle in one punch

К.ФАБЕРЖЕ К.ФАБЕРЖЕ

Fabergé's initials in Cyrillic characters for small objects

КФ

A. v. S.

A Select Bibliography

Basic information on the House of Fabergé can be found in the following books:

Bainbridge, H. C. *Peter Carl Fabergé.* London, 1949, 1966, 1974.
Snowman, A. K. *The Art of Carl Fabergé.* London, 1953, 1962, 1968.
Habsburg-Lothringen, G. v., and A. v. Solodkoff. *Fabergé, Court Jeweller to the Tsars.* London, New York, 1979.

Other recent publications include the following titles:

Snowman, A. K. *Carl Fabergé, Goldsmith to the Imperial Court of Russia.* London, 1979.
Forbes, C. *Fabergé Eggs, Imperial Russian Fantasies.* New York, 1980.
Carl Fabergé and His Contemporaries. Exhibition catalogue. Helsinki: Museum of Applied Arts, 1980.
Solodkoff, A. v. "Fabergé's London Branch." *Connoisseur* February 1982.
Fabergé, Jeweller to Royalty. Exhibition catalogue. New York: Cooper-Hewitt Museum, 1983.
Fabergé. Exhibition catalogue. New York: A la Vieille Russie, 1983.
Lopato, M. "Fresh Light on Fabergé." *Apollo* January 1984.

A. v. S.

Catalogue of the FORBES Magazine Collection

Fantasies

SILVER PRESENTATION PADDLE STEAMER Wigström, 1913. Silver, iodized silver, silver gilt, tinted glass, blue, red, and white enamel; 29 in./740 mm. Inscribed in Cyrillic: *For the Heir Czarevitch, Alexis Nicolaevitch from the Volga Shipbuilders.* Interior musical movement plays *God Save the Czar* and *Sailing Down the Volga.* Ex-collection: Charles Ward; Franklin D. Roosevelt; Elliot Roosevelt; Brandeis University. FAB76021.

SILVER MOTORCAR MODEL Wigström, 1904–05. Silver, red, green, and clear glass; 10¼ in./260 mm. Original wood and glazed case. Fitted as a desk ornament, the steering wheel is a bellpush, the radiator an inkwell, the driver's seat a stamp box, and the passenger's compartment holds pens. This model is thought to have been the mascot of the Imperial Automobile Club. FAB83024.

MINIATURE EMPIRE-STYLE TABLE SET WITH CLOCK Moscow, 1899–1908. Silver gilt, pink enamel, pearls; 3⅜ in./85 mm. FAB79006.

MINIATURE SEDAN CHAIR Perchin, 1899–1903. Gold, salmon pink, sepia, white, and green enamel, rock crystal, mother-of-pearl; 3½ in./85 mm. Ex-collection: J. P. Morgan; Mr. and Mrs. Jack Linsky; Lansdell K. Christie. FAB66007.

MINIATURE RELIQUARY IN THE GOTHIC STYLE Perchin, 1886–99. Nephrite, gold, white and red enamel; 2³/₁₆ in./55 mm. FAB82014.

MINIATURE GUERIDON Moscow, before 1899. Red and green gold, crystal, opals; 2¼ in./56 mm. FAB69001.

MINIATURE SAMOVAR Nevalainen, 1885–1917. Silver gilt, ivory; 3¾ in./96 mm. FAB77003.

MINIATURE SAMOVAR/LIGHTER Nevalainen, 1885–1917. Silver gilt, ebony; 4¾ in./123 mm. FAB83009.

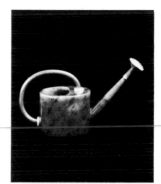

MINIATURE WATERING CAN 1887–1917. Nephrite, diamonds, gold, strawberry red enamel; 4⅛ in./105 mm. Original case. Ex-collection: Mme. Elizabeth Balletta, prima ballerina of the Imperial Michael Theater; Lansdell K. Christie. FAB66008.

MINIATURE COIN TANKARD Kollin, 1870–86. Gold, rubles, sapphires; 3¼ in./85 mm. FAB69004.

MINIATURE BASKET OF LILIES OF THE VALLEY Perchin, 1886–99. Gold, pearls, nephrite; 3⅛ in./80 mm. Ex-collection: Princess Marina, Dowager Duchess of Kent, the granddaughter of Grand Duke Vladimir, brother of Czar Alexander III; Lansdell K. Christie. FAB66012.

MINIATURE WASTEPAPER BASKET Perchin, 1886–99. Two color gold, rubles, white enamel; 1¹³⁄₁₆ in./46 mm. FAB83019.

HOLLY SPRAY Nephrite, purpurine, rock crystal, green gold; 4⅞ in./124 mm. FAB83010.

MINIATURE HELMET CUP 1899–1917. Silver gilt, silver, blue enamel; 3¼ in./85 mm. When inverted the helmet serves as a vodka cup. FAB74005.

DANCING MOUJIK Yellow chalcedony, purpurine, black marble, pink agate, gray jasper, sapphires, gold; 5¼ in./132 mm. Ex-collection: Lansdell K. Christie. FAB66016.

MINIATURE NEPHRITE KOVSH Nephrite, gold, strawberry red enamel, diamonds, pearl; 2½ in./65 mm. Ex-collection: Lansdell K. Christie. FAB76026.

CAPTAIN OF THE 4TH HARKOVSKY LANCERS Wigström, 1914–15. Lapis lazuli, tan and pink agate, obsidian, gold, silver, sapphires, black and yellow enamel; 5 in./125 mm. FAB74004.

HELMET SEAL   Blue and yellow enamel, silver gilt, silver, gold, white agate; 1½ in./38 mm. FAB74003.

AUTOMATED RHINOCEROS 1890–1917. Silver, gold key; 2⅞ in./72 mm. Original case. This rhino is a mate to the one given to Queen Alexandra of England in 1909 for her sixty-fifth birthday by the Lord Chamberlain, Lord Howe. FAB83001.

CRYSTAL POLAR BEAR   Hollming(?), 1876–1915. Rock crystal, rubies; measures 6 in./154 mm. across ice floe. FAB66013.

CRYSTAL ELEPHANT   Rock crystal, rubies; 1⅜ in./35 mm. FAB83011.

PINK RABBIT   1887–1917. Carnelian, diamonds; 1⅛ in./28 mm. Original case. Ex-collection: Czarina Marie Feodorovna; Grand Duchess Xenia, her daughter; Princess Andrew of Russia, her daughter-in-law. Collection of Mrs. Malcolm S. Forbes.

PAIR OF ANGELFISH   Afanassiev, 1908–17. Striated agate, rubies, nephrite, green and red gold; 2⅜ in./62 mm. FAB76029.

OWL IN A CAGE   Perchin, 1899–1903. Gray and brown agate, diamonds, silver gilt, gold, pearls; 4⅛ in./104 mm. FAB83002.

OWL BELL PUSH   Perchin, 1899–1903. Nephrite, tiger's-eye, two color gold; 2⅜ in./60 mm. FAB82013.

OWL SEAL   Wigström, 1886–1917. White chalcedony, rubies, nephrite, gold, diamonds; 2⅛ in./53 mm. FAB68001.

FROG ASHTRAY   Bowenite, gold, garnets; 3½ in./90 mm. Ex-collection: Grand Duke Ernest Ludwig of Hesse and the Rhine, brother of Czarina Alexandra Feodorovna; by descent to the Hon. David Geddes. FAB79009.

Jewelry and Accessories

PIG MATCH HOLDER/STRIKER
First Silver *Artel*, 1908–17. Silver,
sandstone; 6¼ in./158 mm.
FAB83005.

BIG BAD WOLF LIGHTER Rappoport, 1899–1908. Silver, red-
glazed earthenware; 6½ in./164
mm. FAB80003.

EAGLE VASE Alfred Thielemann
or Alexander Tillander, 1870–99.
Silver gilt, blue, turquoise, and red
enamel, gold, diamonds, rubies;
4⅛ in./105 mm. FAB69012.

SMOKEY BEARS ASHTRAY
1903–15. Jasper, demantoids;
6³⁄₁₆ in./156 mm. Original case.
Ex-collection: Prince Youssoupoff. FAB84001.

SCYTHIAN-STYLE BRACELET
Kollin, 1868–99. Gold; 2⁵⁄₁₆ in./
73 mm. Modeled after a bracelet
that was part of the Scythian
treasure, discovered in the second half of the nineteenth century. FAB84003.

ICE PENDANT   1903–13. Rock
crystal, platinum, diamonds; 1³⁄₈
in./85 mm. Purchased by Mr. Oppenheim at the London Branch
of Faberge, December 23, 1913
for £60. FAB80006.

SNOWFLAKE PENDANT WITH
RED CROSS Platinum, diamonds,
rubies, rock crystal, gold; 2¹⁄₁₆ in./
52 mm. FAB81003.

SKETCH OF A PENDANT WITH
IMPERIAL EAGLE 1914–17. *No.
9, K. FABERGÉ, Petrograd*;
Gouache; 4¾ in./120 mm.
FAB82009.

GRISAILLE PIN Albert Holmström, 1914. Pink and grisaille enamel, gold, diamonds; 1½ in./38 mm. Original case. Representing *Winter* after a painting by François Boucher, this image is identical to one of a series of eight grisaille enamels painted by Zuiev which decorate the egg presented to Czarina Marie Feodorovna on Easter 1914. FAB83006.

EDWARD AND ALEXANDRA BROOCH 1901–10. Gold, diamonds, blue-gray enamel; 1⅝ in./41 mm. Edward VII became King of England in 1901. His consort, Alexandra of Denmark, was the sister of Czarina Marie Feodorovna. FAB83004.

NOBEL NECKLACE 1912. Platinum, diamonds, rock crystal, silver; 13⅛ in./333 mm. Original case. Presented to Edla Ahlsell Nobel, by her husband, Dr. Emanuel Nobel, nephew of inventor Alfred Nobel. Portrayed on the medallion are Emanuel Nobel and his father, Ludwig. The reverse is inscribed *1882–1912/Mechanical/Labor/Nobel*. The necklace may also be worn as two bracelets. FAB81004.

BELT BUCKLE WITH QUIVER St. Petersburg, 1899–1908. Gold, white enamel, rubies; 2¼ in./58 mm. FAB73012.

GRAND DUKE KIRILL VLADIMIROVICH CUFF LINKS Hollming, 1908–15. Gold, white enamel, diamonds, rubies; ¾ in./18 mm. Ex-collection: Grand Duke Kirill Vladimirovich, son of Alexander III's brother Vladimir and a member of the Guard Equipage. FAB75002.

OVAL BELT BUCKLE Perchin, 1899–1903. Silver gilt, pink enamel, diamonds; 2¾ in./69 mm. FAB81007.

IMPERIAL CROWN CUFF LINKS 1887–1917. Green gold, white enamel, diamonds; ½ in./13 mm. Original case. Collection of Malcolm S. Forbes.

FIVE BUTTONS HH (unidentified workmaster), 1899–1908. Gold, turquoise blue enamel, diamonds; ⅞ in./23 mm. FAB76024.

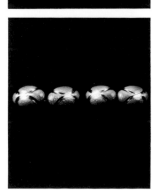

PINK EGG CUFF LINKS Wigström, 1886–99. Gold, pink enamel; ½ in./12 mm. FAB74001.

ROCAILLE OPERA GLASSES Perchin, 1899–1903. Red gold, salmon pink enamel, diamonds; 4¼ in./105 mm. FAB76012.

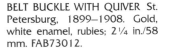

OSTRICH FEATHER FAN Wigström, 1886–1908. Gold, salmon pink enamel, rock crystal, diamonds, mirror, ostrich feathers, silk tassels; 20½ in./530 mm. At the seventeenth-century costume ball at the Winter Palace in February 1903, Grand Duchess Xenia, sister of Czar Nicholas II, is pictured holding such a fan. Ex-collection: Walter Winans, Esq. [purchased from Fabergé London Branch for £90 on 19 September 1908] Peter Otway Smithers, M.P. FAB69007.

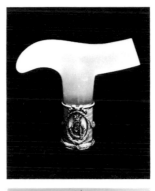

IMPERIAL PARASOL HANDLE 1896–1917. Bowenite, gold, pink and white enamel, diamonds; 2½ in./65 mm. Crowned monogram of Czarina Alexandra Feodorovna. FAB73004.

FESTOONED FAN Wigström, 1899–1908. Gold, salmon pink enamel, diamonds, gauze silk; 8½ in./218 mm. Painted with a *scène galante* by A.E. Begnée. FAB75006.

LOUIS XVI-STYLE PARASOL HANDLE Gold, pink, green, and white enamel, rubies, moonstone, diamonds; 3 in./75 mm. Now mounted as a hand seal. FAB82004.

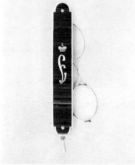

GRAND DUCHESS ELIZABETH LORGNETTE Wigström, 1886–1903. Silver, black, and white enamel; 5 in./126 mm. This lorgnette is applied with the crowned monogram of Grand Duchess Elizabeth, older sister of Czarina Alexandra Feodorovna, who was married to Czar Nicholas II's uncle, Grand Duke Serge. FAB84004.

PINK PARASOL HANDLE Aarne, 1899–1917. Green gold, red gold, pink enamel, moonstone; 2⅜ in./60 mm. Now mounted as a letter opener. FAB76014.

LORGNETTE WITH OCTAGONAL LENSES St. Petersburg, 1899–1908. Red gold, green gold, pink enamel; 5⅞ in./150 mm. Ex-collection: Mrs. L. D. Hirst-Broadhead. FAB69002.

PINK WHISTLE 1890–1917. Silver, silver gilt, pink enamel; 1⅜ in./35 mm. Original case. Ex-collection: Lansdell K. Christie. FAB78003.

HORN LORGNETTE Horn, gold, white enamel, diamonds; 11 in./278 mm. Original case. FAB83015.

BLUE WHISTLE Gold, steel blue enamel; 1⅜ in./34 mm. FAB83026.

KNITTING NEEDLES Wigström, 1886–1917. Ebony, gold, white enamel, chalcedony, rubies; 9⅜ in./238 mm. FAB73001.

HEART SURPRISE FRAME 1897. Gold, strawberry red, green, and white enamel, diamonds, pearls; 3¼ in./82 mm. closed. The frame commemorates the birth in 1897 of Grand Duchess Tatiana whose miniature is flanked by her parents, Czar Nicholas II and Czarina Alexandra Feodorovna. Ex-collection: Lady Lydia Deterding. FAB78004.

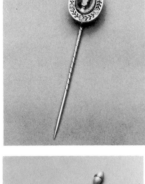

TIE PIN Schramm, before 1899. Gold, black enamel, diamonds, crystal; ¹³⁄₁₆ in./21 mm. without pin. Tinted photo: Czarina Marie Alexandrovna, wife of Czar Alexander II (1824–80). FAB83014.

IMPERIAL REVOLVING FRAME Aarne, 1891–99. Bowenite, silver gilt; 9 in./228 mm. Photos: Sixteen original photos of members of the Russian, Danish, British, and Greek royal families. Ex-collection: Czarina Marie Feodorovna. FAB79012.

LAUREL WREATH SWING FRAME Perchin, 1899–1903. Nephrite, gold, white enamel, pearls; 4¾ in./120 mm. Photo: Czar Alexander III. FAB83007.

HAT PIN Hollming, 1899–1908. Red gold, yellow gold, salmon pink enamel; 7¾ in./197 mm. Original case. FAB83016.

Frames

EASEL FRAME Perchin, 1899–1903. Silver, gold; 8 in./202 mm. Photo: Grand Duchess Xenia holding Ostrich Feather Fan. FAB80005.

FIRE-SCREEN FRAME Wigström, 1914–17. Four color gold, white and pink enamel, pearls; 7⅛ in./180 mm. Photo: Czar Nicholas II (recto), Czarina Alexandra Feodorovna (verso). Original case. Ex-collection: Maurice Sandoz; Lansdell K. Christie. FAB73005.

IMPERIAL PRESENTATION FRAME Perchin, 1899–1903. Gold, rock crystal, pink and green enamel, diamonds, silver gilt, wood; 14⅝ in./372 mm. Original photo: Czar Nicholas II wearing the uniform of the Life Guard Hussars. Original case. Presented by Czar Alexander III to his wife, Marie Feodorovna, whose monogram decorates the frame. Ex-collection: Maurice Sandoz. FAB65003.

KAISER WILHELM II FRAME Nevalainen, 1899–1908. Two color silver gilt, pale blue enamel, wood; 11¾ in./298 mm. Photo: Kaiser Wilhelm II of Germany, autographed and inscribed *Berlin, Feb. 1909*. FAB76008.

VIEUX ROSE FRAME Armfeldt, 1899–1908. Green gold, red gold, vieux rose enamel, pearls, ivory; 2⅞ in./75 mm. Photo: Czar Nicholas II. FAB76017.

PALE BLUE FRAME Nevalainen, 1899–1908. Silver, silver gilt, pale blue enamel, wood; 8¼ in./210 mm. Photographic postcard of Czarevitch Alexis sent by Czarina Alexandra to Princess Marie Bariatinsky, her lady-in-waiting. FAB76031.

WHITE FRAME Perchin, 1899–1903. Green gold, red gold, white and green enamel, diamonds, ivory; 2¾ in./70 mm. Photo: Czarevitch Alexis. FAB76018.

MARIE PAVLOVNA MIRROR Aarne, 1899–1908. Silver, silver gilt, scarlet and white enamel, diamonds, mirror, wood; 8⅞ in./226 mm. The monogram of Grand Duchess Marie Pavlovna (1854–1920), a Princess of Mecklenburg, who married Grand Duke Vladimir Alexandrovich, brother of Alexander III in 1874. FAB77002.

LAUREL-SPRIG FRAME Perchin, 1886–99. Red gold, green gold, pink and white enamel, tortoiseshell; 4 in./102 mm. Photo: Czar Nicholas II. FAB75001.

LATTICE-WORK FRAME Aarne, 1891–99. Four color gold, scarlet and white enamel, pearls; 4¼ in./115 mm. Photo: Czar Nicholas II. FAB73002.

AMATORY FRAME Perchin, 1886–99. Four color gold, pink enamel, ivory; 4⅛ in./105 mm. Photo: Czarina Marie Feodorovna and her sister, Queen Alexandra of England. FAB76001.

CRYSTAL FRAME Perchin, 1899–1903. Rock crystal, four color gold, diamonds, rubies, pink enamel, ivory; 4 in./102 mm. Photo: Grand Duchess Marie, third daughter of Czar Nicholas II. FAB74006.

MINIATURE PINK FRAME Aarne, 1899–1908. Four color gold, pink enamel, pearls, silver gilt, mother-of-pearl; 1¾ in./44 mm. Original case. Photo: Czarina Alexandra Feodorovna. FAB78007.

MAUVE FRAME Aarne, 1891–1908. Gold, mauve enamel, ivory; 2⁵/₁₆ in./57 mm. Photo: Czarina Alexandra Feodorovna holding Grand Duchess Tatiana. FAB84002.

Presentation and Commemorative Commissions

CIRCULAR SOFTWOOD FRAME Nevalainen, 1899–1908. Wood, silver, silver gilt; 6½ in./164 mm. Ex-collection: Czarina Marie Feodorovna; Grand Duchess Xenia (whose photograph the frame contains), sister of Czar Nicholas II; Prince Dimitri. FAB79011.

IMPERIAL PRESENTATION TRAY Wigström, 1899–1908. Nephrite, two color gold, strawberry red enamel, diamonds; 23⅜ in./593 mm. Original case. The handles are mounted with the crowned monograms of Czar Nicholas II and Czarina Alexandra Feodorovna. FAB79007.

KARELIAN BIRCH FRAME Nevalainen, 1899–1908. Karelian birch, silver gilt; 5½ in./140 mm. Original photo: Czarevitch Alexis. Verso scratched *Spala 1912* by Czarina Alexandra Feodorovna who presented it to her sister, Princess Irene of Hesse, wife of Prince Henry of Prussia. FAB76016.

IMPERIAL WRITING PORTFOLIO Perchin, 1886–99. Leather, silver gilt, diamonds, watered silk; 12½ in./335 mm. Applied with the crowned double monogram of Czar Nicholas II and Czarina Alexandra Feodorovna. Inscribed in Cyrillic: *From the City of St. Petersburg.* FAB74002.

SILVER ANNIVERSARY ICON Armfeldt, 1913. Silver, wood, pearls; 6½ in./164 mm. open. Original case. A twenty-fifth wedding anniversary present to Princess Cantacuzene from Princess Youssoupoff, 1913. The painted icons represent Our Lady of Protection (center), St. Sophie (left), and St. Matthew (right). FAB81005.

LARGE WOOD FRAME Rappoport, 1908–16. Wood, silver gilt, blue enamel; 13¼ in./337 mm. Photo: Czar Nicholas II and Czarina Alexandra Feodorovna. FAB76007.

RYURIK PLAQUE Nevalainen, 1905. Silver, rosewood; 8¼ in./208 mm. Original case. Inscribed in Cyrillic: *Made to Commemorate the Launching of the Cruiser.* The reverse lists the names of persons involved with design and construction of the cruiser. An identical plaque is in the Marjorie Merriweather Post Collection at Hillwood; Several others have appeared at auction. FAB79014.

MONUMENTAL BOGATYR KOVSH Moscow, 1899–1908. Silver, silver gilt, semiprecious stones; 23 in./582 mm. Original case. *Bogatyrs* were the legendary warriors of medieval Russia. FAB81001.

BRICK MATCH HOLDER WITH SATYRS Silver, terra cotta. Brick: Gusarev Factory, Moscow. 4¾ in./120 mm. Original case. Another Fabergé silver-mounted Gusarev brick, signed Eric Kollin, before 1899, is reproduced in A. Kenneth Snowman, *Carl Fabergé, Goldsmith to the Imperial Court of Russia*, p. 46. FAB82001.

GRAND DUKE KIRILL VLADI-MIROVICH KOVSH Moscow, 1899–1908. Silver, silver gilt, amethysts; 8½ in./205 mm. Inscribed on the front: *1914/Prize/August Patronage/Teriokski Naval Yacht Club of His Imperial Majesty Grand Duke Kirill Vladimirovich.* Ex-collection: Grand Duke Kirill Vladimirovich, son of Alexander III's brother Vladimir and a member of the Guard Equipage. FAB83025.

Boxes

REGIMENTAL PRESENTATION TROPHY Rappoport, c. 1912. Silver; 22½ in./570 mm. Thought to have been presented on the occasion of the centenary of Napoleon's retreat from Moscow. FAB79005.

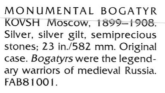

CORONATION BOX Holmström, 1896–99. Gold, gold and black enamel, diamonds; 3¾ in./95 mm. Original case. Presented by Czarina Alexandra Feodorovna to her husband, Czar Nicholas II, Easter 1897, the year he gave her the Coronation Egg. Ex-collection: Herr Bomm; Sidney Hill; Arthur E. Bradshaw; Lansdell K. Christie. FAB66009.

WAR PRESENTATION BEAKER Wigström, 1915. Nephrite, silver; 3⅞ in./97 mm. Medallions embossed with Imperial Eagle and the inscription *WAR/1914–1915/K. FABERGE.* FAB80002.

ROCAILLE BOX Perchin, 1886–99. Gold, royal blue and white enamel, diamonds; 3¾ in./95 mm. The surprise miniature of Czar Nicholas II is concealed under his monogram. Ex-collection: H. Blum. FAB78005.

BADGE OF THE BROTHERHOOD OF THE HOLY GHOST OF THE TRINITY Rappoport, 1909. Silver gilt, white and blue enamel, gold, silver; 3¼ in./85 mm. Inscribed in Cyrillic on verso: *Emblem of the Vilna Brotherhood of the Holy Ghost of the Trinity, 1909.* Ex-collection: Richard R. Draper. FAB67002.

NICHOLAS II NEPHRITE BOX Wigström, 1915–17. Nephrite, diamonds, green gold; 3¾ in./95 mm. Miniaturist: Zuiev. Original case. Ex-collection: Mrs. J. M. Jacques; Lansdell K. Christie. FAB66021.

CASTENSKIOLD IMPERIAL PRESENTATION CIGARETTE CASE Holmström, before 1899. Gold, royal blue enamel, diamonds, paste brilliants; 3¾ in./95 mm. Presented by Czar Nicholas II to Ludwig Castenskiold, Equerry of the Czar's great-uncle, King Christian IX of Denmark. FAB82012.

RÜCKERT CIGARETTE CASE Rückert, 1908–17. Silver, moss green, blue, and aubergine enamel, sapphire; 3¾ in./94 mm. Original case. In the Pan-Slavic or Old Russian Style. FAB83018.

GOLD IMPERIAL PRESENTATION CIGARETTE CASE Niukkanen, 1899–1908. Gold, diamonds, sapphire; 3¾ in./95 mm. Collection of Mrs. Malcolm S. Forbes.

SQUARE NEPHRITE BOX Wigström, 1886–1917. Nephrite, green gold, strawberry red enamel, diamonds; 3¾ in./95 mm. FAB79001.

WAR PRESENTATION CIGARETTE CASE 1914–15. Copper, brass; 3³⁄₁₆ in./80 mm. Raised Cyrillic characters on lid: *WAR/1914–1915/K.FABERGÉ*. Numerous "austerity" pieces such as this and the War Presentation Beaker were presented to Russian officers by the Czar. FAB81006.

LOUIS XVI-STYLE SNUFFBOX Perchin, 1886–99. Gold, green, red, and white enamel, diamonds; 3¼ in./82 mm. The painted enamel plaque represents *Venus and Cupid*. Ex-collection: Czar Nicholas II, Alexander's son; Lansdell K. Christie. FAB66020.

TORTOISESHELL CIGARETTE CASE 1899–1908. Tortoiseshell, platinum, gold, diamonds; 3¹⁄₁₆ in./77 mm. Decorated with flowering mustard-seed motifs in the Art Nouveau style. FAB82005.

BOX WITH VIEWS OF THE FORTRESS OF ST. PETER AND ST. PAUL Wigström, 1899–1908. Gold, oyster rose, white, green, and sepia enamel, diamonds, pearls; 2¼ in./57 mm. Ex-collection: Mlle. Yznaga, sister of the Duchess of Manchester. FAB82006.

ART DECO CIGARETTE CASE Moscow, before 1899. Gold, oyster pink, salmon pink, brown, royal blue, blue gray, rust, green, olive green, yellow, and taupe enamel, diamonds, sapphire. 3½ in./88 mm. FAB83023.

LOVE TROPHY BONBONNIÈRE Perchin, 1886–99. Gold, blue, and white enamel, crystal, diamonds; 1⅝ in./42 mm. FAB76027.

VIAL WITH ROSE TRELLIS LID
Wigström, 1886–1917. Rock
crystal, gold, pink, and green
enamel, diamonds; 1½ in./38
mm. FAB82003.

IVAN THE TERRIBLE DESK SET
Pen rest, Moscow, 1899–1917.
Silver, crystal, gemstone.

VINAIGRETTE Moscow, 1899–
1908. Gold, turquoise blue, and
dark green enamel, diamonds; ⅞
in./21 mm. FAB76023.

IVAN THE TERRIBLE DESK SET
Seal, Moscow, 1899–1917.
Silver, crystal, gemstone.

Desk Pieces

IVAN THE TERRIBLE DESK SET
Letter opener, Moscow, 1899–
1917. Silver, crystal, gemstone.

IVAN THE TERRIBLE DESK SET
Inkwell, Moscow, 1899–1917.
Silver, crystal, gemstone. Ex-collection: Nikolai Roerich. Roerich
(1874–1947) was a historical
painter and may have designed
this desk set, which represents
Ivan the Terrible and the Boyars
in the Old Russian Style.
FAB83013.

PERPETUAL CALENDAR Per-
chin, 1886–99. Nephrite, moonstones, silver gilt, yellow gold, lin-
en; 5¾ in./143 mm. FAB65008.

IVAN THE TERRIBLE DESK SET
Pair of lamps, Moscow, 1899–
1917. Silver, crystal, gemstone.

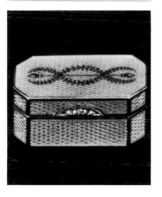

DESK PAD Moscow, 1899–
1908. Nephrite, silver gilt, white
enamel, green gold, red gold,
garnets; 5½ in./126 mm.
FAB76032.

CARD HOLDER ON BUN FEET Perchin, 1899–1903. Nephrite, red gold, green gold; 3 in./75 mm. FAB76013.

PEN TRAY Perchin, 1886–99. Bowenite, gold, scarlet and white enamel; 6½ in./168 mm. FAB73006.

HVIDØRE SEAL Perchin, 1886–99. Nephrite, carnelian, two color gold; 2¼ in./55 mm. Ex-collection: Czarina Marie Feodorovna; Grand Duchess Xenia, her daughter; Prince Vassily Romanov, her son; Marina Beadleston, his daughter-in-law. The matrix was cut after the purchase in 1905 (or 1906?) of the Hvidøre (White Ear) Villa outside Copenhagen by the Danish Dowager Empress Marie and her sister, Queen Alexandra of England. FAB77001.

LAPIS LAZULI SEAL Lapis lazuli, gold, peach, white, and green enamel, diamonds; 3½ in./90 mm. FAB73009.

BLOODSTONE GLUE POT Wigström, 1899–1908. Bloodstone, two color gold, white enamel, diamonds, pearls, sable; 3⁹/₁₆ in./9 mm. Ex-collection: Mrs. Robert Tritton. FAB83012.

GLUE POT Wigström, 1899–1908. Silver gilt, green gold, red gold, oyster enamel, garnet, sable; 2 in./51 mm. Original case. FAB79004.

SERPENT PEN Perchin, 1886–99. Nephrite, gold, diamonds, rubies; 7 in./177 mm. excluding nib. FAB65009.

BOOTJACK PEN REST Nephrite, gold, ruby; 1¹¹/₁₆ in./42 mm. Original case. FAB80010.

GRAND DUCHESS OLGA PAPER KNIFE St. Petersburg, 1899–1908. Nephrite, red gold, green gold, strawberry red enamel, diamond; 9 in./228 mm. Original case. Miniature of Grand Duchess Olga, sister of Czar Nicholas II. FAB76005.

NEPHRITE PAPER KNIFE Nephrite, green gold, salmon pink and white enamel; 3³/₈ in./98 mm. Ex-collection: Mrs. L.D. Hirst-Broadhead. FAB69003.

SQUARE MAGNIFYING GLASS Perchin, 1899–1903. Gold, green enamel, diamonds, moonstone; 3¹⁵/₁₆ in./99 mm. Presented by Queen Mary to her surgeon, Sir Russell Wilkenson, K.C.V.O.; Jeremy Grantham, by descent. FAB80009.

TRAVELING PENCIL Soloviev, 1908–17. Gold; 3 in./75 mm. FAB80004.

ROUND MAGNIFYING GLASS Wigström, 1899–1908. Green gold, red enamel; 3¹/₁₆ in./78 mm. Ex-collection: Mrs. L.D. Hirst-Broadhead. FAB69009.

Household Objects

BOOK BLADE AND LOOP Perchin, 1886–99. Green gold, red gold, pink enamel, rock crystal, rubies; 4 in./102 mm. Ex-collection: H.M. King Farouk of Egypt; Robert Strauss. FAB76015.

POLAR STAR CLOCK Perchin, 1886–99. Gold, white, black, pink, and sepia enamel, nephrite, silver, ivory, diamonds; 5¼ in./132 mm. Original case. Thought to have been made for the Imperial Yacht, Polar Star Ex-collection: Dr. and Mrs. Leonard Slotover. FAB83027.

ROCK CRYSTAL BOOKMARK Perchin, 1886–99. Gold, rock crystal, pink enamel, pearl; 2⁷/₈ in./73 mm. Ex-collection: Mrs. L.D. Hirst-Broadhead. FAB69010.

TWENTY-FIFTH ANNIVERSARY CLOCK Wigström. Nephrite, pink and pale blue enamel, diamonds, pearls, silver gilt, green gold, red gold; 6 in./166 mm. Ex-collection: Mr. and Mrs. C. J. Byrne. FAB69008.

FLEUR-DE-LYS BOOKMARK Perchin, 1886–99. Bowenite, gold, strawberry red enamel, diamonds; 3¼ in./82 mm. Presented by Queen Mary to her surgeon, Sir Russell Wilkenson, K.C.V.O.; Jeremy Grantham, by descent. FAB80008.

PEDESTAL CLOCK Nephrite, silver gilt; 6⁷/₈ in./174 mm. FAB80007.

STYLE-MODERNE CLOCK Wigström, 1907. Gold, pink, white, dark blue, and black enamel, silver, seed pearls; 5 in./126 mm. The dedication plaque is inscribed in Cyrillic: *Murochka/on her birthday/18 May 1907/ Mirra.* FAB84005.

STANDING THERMOMETER Aarne, 1899–1908. Silver gilt, gold, pink and white enamel, wood, glass; 4⅞ in./123 mm. FAB82011.

ROUND BELL PUSH Perchin, 1899–1903. Bowenite, green gold, salmon pink enamel, diamonds, pearls, moonstone; 2¼ in./58 mm. FAB76009.

IVAN KALITA BOWL Moscow, 1899–1908. Silver, silver gilt, emeralds, ruby; 6¼ in./158 mm. The Ivan caricatured here became Prince of Moscow in 1325 and Grand Duke of Russia from 1339–41. His miserliness earned him the sobriquet "Kalita" (Moneybags). Ex-collection: Irving M. Feldstein. FAB83017.

OVAL BELL PUSH Bowenite, gold, white enamel, diamonds, garnet; 2¾ in./71 mm. FAB65005.

RHODONITE ASHTRAY WITH RUBLES Afanassiev, 1899–1908. Rhodonite, gold, white and green enamel, rubles; 6¾ in./170 mm. Ex-collection: Mrs. Isabella Catt. FAB69006.

PAIR OF TOILET BOTTLES Moscow, 1899–1908. Cut glass, gold, pale blue enamel, amethysts, diamonds; 5⅛ in./130 mm. FAB82016.

CIRCULAR PINK AGATE ASHTRAY Wigström, 1899–1908. Pink agate, gold, green enamel; 2¾ in./79 mm. FAB65004.

SILVER-MOUNTED CRACKLED GLASS VASE Perchin, 1886–99. Silver gilt, glass; 4⅛ in./104 mm. Vase: E. Léviellé, Paris. FAB82002.

CIRCULAR BOWENITE ASHTRAY Perchin, 1899–1903. Bowenite, gold, rubies; 3½ in./89 mm. FAB76025.

SQUARE BOWENITE ASHTRAY
Wigström, 1908–17. Bowenite,
gold, white and deep blue enamel; 2⅞ in./74 mm. Original case.
FAB00001.

CARD-SUIT ASHTRAYS Mos-
cow, 1899–1908. Silver gilt,
gold, white, red, and blue enamel; largest piece: 3⅝ in./92 mm.
Original case. Ex-collection: Mrs.
Hugh J. Chisholm, Jr. FAB73003.

ART NOUVEAU MATCH HOLD-
ER Wigström, 1886–1917. Jasper, gold, demantoids, rubies;
2⅝ in./68 mm. FAB00002.

IMPERIAL CYLINDER VASE Wigström, 1899–1908. Nephrite,
gold, rubies, diamonds; 4⅝ in./
117 mm. FAB76011.

STYLE MODERNE KOVSH
1903–15. Nephrite, gold, white
enamel, moonstones; 5 in./128
mm. Original case. FAB65006.

FIGUREHEAD KOVSH Kollin,
1870–86. Bowenite, gold, diamonds, pearl, moonstone; 4½
in./114 mm. Ex-collection: Theo-
dore Case. FAB79013.

RENAISSANCE-STYLE AGATE
KOVSH Perchin, 1886–99. Striated agate, gold, green, white,
blue, orange, yellow, and black
enamel, diamonds; 4½ in./112
mm. FAB 76020.

FISH CHARKA Perchin, 1886–
99. Red gold, white gold, ruble,
sapphire, rubies; 3½ in./88 mm.
FAB77004.

SIX VODKA CHARKI (two of the
set) Perchin, 1886–99. Gold,
strawberry red and white enamel, glass, rubies; 1¾ in./44 mm.
Original case. The *charki* (cups)
are in the form of miniature tea
glasses. Ex-collection: H. Harris.
FAB82007.

VODKA CUP WITH RUBIES Perchin, 1899–1903. Red gold,
green gold, yellow gold, rubies;
1⅞ in./48 mm. FAB65012.

VODKA CUP WITH SAPPHIRES Perchin, 1899–1903. Red gold, green gold, yellow gold, sapphires; 1⅞ in./48 mm. FAB65010.

DECANTER STOPPER Aarne, 1899–1908. Silver, cork; 4½ in./ 115 mm. Made in the Imperial Glass Factory in first quarter of the nineteenth century. The decanter for which this stopper is a replacement is etched with a portrait and monogram of Czar Alexander I. FAB76030.

SMALL VODKA CUP WITH SAPPHIRES Perchin, 1886–99. Red gold, green gold, yellow gold, sapphires; 1¹³⁄₁₆ in./45 mm. Ex-collection: H. M. King Farouk of Egypt; Major W. Heaford Daubney. FAB82008.

CHRISTENING SET Alexander Wäkevä, 1915–17. Silver, glass; Largest piece: 5½ in./139 mm. Original case. FAB82010.

TUMBLE CUP Moscow, 1908–17. Silver gilt, black, olive green, royal blue, light blue, white, yellow, pink, and beige enamel; 1½ in./37 mm. In the Pan-Slavic style, this piece retains its original paper Fabergé label. FAB81002.

Miniature Eggs

MINIATURE EGGS 1⅛ in./30 mm. largest; ⅝ in./16 mm. smallest.

EMPIRE-STYLE SILVER AND SILVER GILT TABLE SERVICE Moscow, 1908–17. Silver gilt, silver, steel blades; 370 pieces; largest piece: 13 in./329 mm. FAB79010 and FAB80001.

HELMET EGG Purpurine, black and red enamel, gold, silver. The helmet is that of Her Majesty's Guard Lancers. Ex-collection: Lansdell K. Christie. FAB66011G.

FOUR MENU HOLDERS (two of the set) Nevalainen, 1899–1908. Silver gilt, pale blue enamel, wood; 2⅜ in./61 mm. Ex-collection: Mrs. R. L. Cameron. FAB76028.

WHITE EGG IN ART NOUVEAU STYLE Perchin, 1886–1903. White enamel, gold, rubies. FAB73007.

ROMANOV CROWN PENDANT EGG Knut Oskar Pihl, 1887–97. Purpurine, gold, rubies, diamonds. FAB00005.

IMPERIAL EAGLE EGG Wigström, 1886–1917. Rhodonite, silver, gold. FAB78013.

CANNON EGG Alfred Thielemann or Alexander Tillander, Jr. Silver, rhodonite. FAB00008.

ANCHORS EGG Kollin, 1899–1908. Blue enamel, gold, Ex-collection: Lansdell K. Christie. FAB66011E.

ROMANOV BANNER EGG Afanassiev. Black, yellow, red, white, and blue enamel, gold. Ex-collection: Lansdell K. Christie. FAB66011B.

IMPERIAL NAVY EGG Gold, blue, red, and white enamel Ex-collection: Grand Duke Alexis Alexandrovich, Grand Admiral of the Imperial Russian Navy. FAB83008.

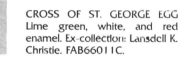

UNION JACK EGG Lundell, 1899–1908. White, blue, and red enamel, gold. Ex-collection: Lansdell K. Christie. FAB66011D.

CROSS OF ST. GEORGE EGG Lime green, white, and red enamel. Ex-collection: Lansdell K. Christie. FAB66011C.

RED CROSS EGG White and red enamel, gold. The Czarina and her daughters worked for the Red Cross during World War I. Ex-collection: Lansdell K. Christie. FAB66011A.

RED CROSS EGG Hollming, 1880–1915. White and red enamel, gold. Collection of Mrs. Malcolm S. Forbes.

EASTER BUNNY EGG Holmström, 1899–1903. Gold, aventurine quartz. Original case. FAB83020.

CHICK IN AN EGG-SHAPED PERCH Afanassiev. Amethystine quartz, gold, diamonds. FAB75005.

KINGFISHER EGG Brown and green hardstone, gold, diamonds. FAB83021.

MUSHROOM BASKET EGG Gold, mottled brown and ivory enamel. FAB79008.

LADYBUG EGG Perchin, 1886–1903. Green gold, yellow gold, black and red enamel. FAB78012.

SWAN BASKET EGG Wigström, 1899–1908. Gold, colored stones. FAB68002.

FISH EGG Oxidized gold, gold, rubies, pearl. FAB75004.

CHICK EGG Blue, yellow, orange, and white enamel, gold. FAB00009.

EGG-SHAPED CHICK WITH SWING Wigström, 1886-1917. Green jasper, gold, rubies. FAB83003.

PRIMROSE EGG White, green, and yellow enamel, gold. Ex-collection: a grand-daughter of Grand Duchess Marie Alexandrovich, Duchess of Edinburgh. FAB82015.

ACORN EGG Wigström, 1886–1917. Nephrite, diamonds, gold. FAB00013.

TRELLIS-WORK FRAME EGG Alfred Thielemann, 1880–1910. Platinum, gold, diamonds, sapphires. Period photograph. FAB79015.

RASPBERRY EGG Kollin, 1899–1908. Rubies, gold. FAB00003.

DUCAL CORONET EGG Perchin, 1899–1903. White, yellow, and salmon enamel, gold, diamonds. FAB68004.

RIBBON EGG Perchin, 1886–1903. Gold, diamonds, silver, royal blue enamel. FAB78009.

FLEUR-DE-LYS EGG Auburn enamel, gold. FAB00006.

TRIPLET EGG Perchin, 1886–1903. Gold, lilac, raspberry, and royal blue enamel. FAB78010.

MOSS AGATE EGG Wigström, 1899–1908. Pink and sepia enamel, gold, diamonds. Ex-collection: H.R.H. The Princess Royal, great-niece of Czarina Marie Feodorovna. FAB66022.

EGG WITHIN EGG LOOP Wigström, 1886–99. Yellow gold, red gold, russet and white enamel. FAB78011.

LOUIS XVI-STYLE EGG 1899–1908. Blue and white enamel, green gold, red gold. FAB00007.

184

RF 1900 EGG Alexander Tillander, 1900. Green enamel, gold. Ex-collection: Lansdell K. Christie. FAB66011I.

ART NOUVEAU EGG Perchin(?), 1886–1903. Green gold, red gold, rubies, sapphire. FAB78008.

RF 1903 EGG Knut Oskar Pihl(?), 1903. Yellow enamel, gold. Ex-collection: Lansdell K. Christie. FAB66011H.

PEARL TREFOIL EGG Reimar(?), 1870–98. Gold, pearls, diamond. FAB00011.

CASTELLATED PINK AND GREEN EGG Alfred Thielemann, 1880–1910. Pink and green enamel, gold, diamonds. FAB66018.

REEDED EGG Perchin, 1886–1903. Two color gold, paste brilliants. FAB00012.

CASTELLATED WHITE AND BLUE EGG Alfred Thielemann, 1880–1910. White and blue enamel, gold, diamonds. Ex-collection: Anna Lois Webber. FAB66017.

PAVÉ-SET JEWELLED EGG Wigström, 1886–99. Gold, diamonds, emeralds. FAB67003.

WHITE EGG WITH A SQUARE CUT RUBY White enamel, gold, ruby. Ex-collection: Lansdell K. Christie. FAB66011F.

ROCOCO TRELLIS EGG Hollming, 1880–1915. Gold, crystal. FAB00010.

185

BIRCH EGG Birch, sapphire, yellow gold. FAB78014.

BANDED NEPHRITE EGG Wigström, 1886–1917. Nephrite, gold, diamonds. FAB83022.

NEPHRITE EGG Nephrite, gold. FAB68003A.

GUN-METAL BLUE EGG Gunmetal blue enamel, gold. Ex-collection: Lansdell K. Christie. FAB66011J.

ROYAL BLUE EGG Royal blue enamel, gold. Ex-collection: Lansdell K. Christie. FAB66011K.

AUBERGINE EGG Aarne, 1891–99. Aubergine enamel, gold. Ex-collection: Lansdell K. Christie. FAB66011L.

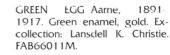

GREEN EGG Aarne, 1891–1917. Green enamel, gold. Ex-collection: Lansdell K. Christie. FAB66011M.

Other Eggs

DUCHESS OF MARLBOROUGH EGG Perchin, 1902. Gold, pink, and white enamel, pearls, diamonds, four color gold; 9¼ in./235 mm. Original case. Purchased on the occasion of the visit of the Duke and Duchess of Marlborough to Russia in 1902. The Duchess was American-born heiress Consuelo Vanderbilt. Ex-collection: Mme. Ganna Walska. FAB65001.

KELCH HEN EGG Perchin, 1898. Gold, strawberry red and white enamel, diamonds, rubies, suede; 3¼ in./84 mm. Surprise: hinged yolk: gold, yellow enamel. Opens to reveal a removable hen: gold, brown, white, and yellow enamel; 1⅜ in./35 mm., within which is a removable folding easel: gold, diamonds, rubies; 1⅛ in./56 mm., with a miniature of Czarevitch Alexis. Original case. Ex-collection: Lansdell K. Christie. FAB66006.

RABBIT EGG Perchin, 1899–1903. Silver gilt, green gold, yellow enamel; 2 in./50 mm. without stand: gold, red enamel, ruble. Surprise: removable rabbit: pink chalcedony, demantoids; 1⅛ in./38 mm. Ex-collection: Lansdell K. Christie. FAB66015.

Imperial Eggs

HOOF EGG Perchin, 1886–99. Bowenite, red gold, diamonds, rubies, pearls; 3¼ in./83 mm. open. The miniature is of Czarina Alexandra Feodorovna. FAB66003.

FIRST IMPERIAL EGG Kollin(?), 1885. Gold, white enamel; 2½ in./64 mm. Surprise: removable yolk: gold, 1⁹⁄₁₆ in./40 mm. Opens to reveal a hen: four color gold, rubies; 1⅜ in./35 mm., which in turn contained further surprises, now lost. Presented by Czar Alexander III to his wife, Marie Feodorovna, Easter 1885. Ex-collection: Lady Grantchester. FAB78001.

EGG BONBONNIÈRE Wigström, 1899–1908. Silver gilt, white, sepia, pale blue enamel, rubies, diamonds, red gold, green gold; 1⅞ in./48 mm. Ex-collection: Mrs. L. Turnbull. FAB65007.

RESURRECTION EGG Perchin, 1889(?). Rock crystal, gold, red, white, blue, green, yellow, and beige enamel, diamonds, pearls; 3⅞ in./98 mm. Presented by Czar Alexander III to his wife, Marie Feodorovna, Easter 1889 (?). Ex-collection: Lady Grantchester. FAB78002.

CIGARETTE HOLDER EGG Wigström, 1908–1917. Two color gold, white enamel, diamonds; 1³⁄₁₆ in./30 mm. The egg opens to reveal a telescoping cigarette holder. FAB83028.

RENAISSANCE EGG Perchin, 1894. White agate, gold, green, red, blue, black, and white enamel, diamonds, rubies; 5¼ in./140 mm. Original case. Presented by Czar Alexander III to his wife, Marie Feodorovna, Easter 1894. Ex-collection: H.T. de Vere Clifton; Mr. and Mrs. Jack Linsky. FAB66001.

SCENT FLACON EGG Wigström, 1886–1917. Gold, blue enamel, diamonds, moonstone; 1¼ in./32 mm. Ex-collection: Lansdell K. Christie. FAB66010.

CORONATION EGG Perchin and Wigström, 1897. Gold, lime yellow, and black enamel, diamonds; 5 in./126 mm. Surprise: removable miniature replica by George Stein of the coronation coach: gold, platinum, strawberry red enamel, diamonds, rubies, rock crystal; 3¹¹⁄₁₆ in./93 mm. Presented by Czar Nicholas II to his wife, Alexandra Feodorovna, Easter 1897, the first Easter following their coronation. FAB79002.

LILIES OF THE VALLEY EGG Perchin, 1898. Gold, pink, and green enamel, diamonds, rubies, pearls; 7⅞ in./200 mm. (open). Surprise: miniatures painted by Zehngraf of Czar Nicholas II and his two eldest daughters, Olga and Tatiana, which rise out of the egg when a geared mechanism is activated by turning a pearl "button." Original case. Presented by Nicholas II to his mother, Marie Feodorovna, Easter 1898. FAB79003.

CROSS OF ST. GEORGE EGG 1916. Silver, gold, opalescent white, rose, pale green, white, orange, and black enamel; 3⁵/₁₆ in./90 mm. without stand. Surprise: miniatures of Czar Nicholas II and his son, Czarevitch Alexis. Original case. Presented by Czar Nicholas II to his mother, Marie Feodorovna, Easter 1916. Ex-collection: Grand Duchess Xenia; Prince Vassily Romanov, her son; Fabergé Inc. FAB76010.

SPRING FLOWERS EGG Perchin, before 1899. Green gold, red gold, platinum, strawberry red enamel, bowenite; 3¼ in./83 mm. Surprise: removable basket of wood anemones: platinum, gold, green enamel, white chalcedony, demantoids; 1½ in./33 mm. Original case. Presented by Czar Alexander III to his wife, Marie Feodorovna, Easter 1886–92. Ex-collection: Lansdell K. Christie. FAB66004.

CHANTICLEER EGG Perchin, 1903(?). Green gold, red gold, Cambridge blue, white, green, red, orange, and yellow enamel, pearls, diamonds; 12⅝ in./320 mm. open. Original silver key. Surprise: a chanticleer which emerges crowing and flapping its wings on the hour. Possibly presented by Czar Nicholas II to his mother, Marie Feodorovna, Easter 1903. Ex-collection: Maurice Sandoz; Lansdell K. Christie. FAB66005.

FIFTEENTH ANNIVERSARY EGG 1911. Gold, green, white, and oyster enamel, ivory, diamonds, crystal; 5⅛ in./132 mm. without stand. Miniaturist: Zuiev. Original case. Presented by Czar Nicholas II to his wife, Alexandra Feodorovna, Easter 1911. The egg commemorates the fifteenth anniversary of the coronation and the miniatures depict the Czar and Czarina, their children, and major events of the reign. FAB66023.

ORANGE TREE EGG 1911. Gold, nephrite, diamonds, citrines, amethysts, agate, rubies, pearls, white and green enamel, feathers; 11¾ in./300 mm. open. Gold key. Surprise: concealed within is a mechanical bird which emerges singing when the right "orange" is turned. Presented by Czar Nicholas II to his mother, Marie Feodorovna, Easter 1911. Ex-collection: A. G. Hughes; Arthur E. Bradshaw; W. Magalow; Maurice Sandoz; Mildred Kaplan. FAB65002.

Acknowledgments

This book is the result of the happy cooperation of a number of great people and institutions, the exceptional contributions of a few of whom it gives me great pleasure to acknowledge here.

To *Alexander von Solodkoff,* whose ongoing scholarship makes it possible to publish here so many new discoveries about the masterpieces of the House of Fabergé. His own acknowledgments appear below.

To *Paul Schaffer* and *Kenneth Snowman,* scholar-dealers who share some fascinating reminiscences of the early days of their great firms. Without Paul Schaffer, his brother Peter, mother Ray and late father Alexander, as well as Kenneth Snowman, so many of the splendid objects illustrating this book would not now belong to FORBES Magazine.

To *Roy Betteley* for his fascinating essay on the Fabergé collection assembled by the Kings of Siam. Those who helped in his research are noted below.

To *Marilyn Swezey,* whose knowledge of Czarist history and the Russian language has been invaluable to us over the years, which in turn makes her essay on Nicholas II's reign, as chronicled in the Fifteenth Anniversary Egg, so interesting.

To *Margaret Kelly,* FORBES Magazine Curator for over a decade, whose own expertise on Fabergé is becoming ever more widely acknowledged. Without her and her assistants, this book would never have been pulled together. Most particularly, *Barbara Pollack,* who single-handedly produced the catalogue of the FORBES Magazine Collection. Also for her help in many ways, *Mary Ellen Adamo.*

As scintillating as is the text, no book on Fabergé can capture the genius of the master without brilliant photographs. Chief among those responsible for the dazzling images commissioned especially for this book are *Larry Stein* and his assistant *June Greenman.* Also, our thanks to *Robert Wharton* and *Otto Nelson,* as well as the many others who allowed us to use their photographs and whose names appear in the photocredits.

The metamorphosis of hundreds of pages of typescript and equal numbers of photographs into the sumptuous volume before you has been the work of an entire team at *Harry N. Abrams, Inc., Publishers.* Most notably among them, "Team Captain" editor *Darlene Geis,* who encouraged, inspired, prodded, and patiently brought it all together and *Darilyn Lowe,* whose design and layout are as carefully crafted, and the result as stunning, as any of Fabergé's masterpieces.

Finally, to my assistant, *Ronni Pring,* who does most of my work but still lets me take the credit.

C. F.

For information and help while writing this study, I am grateful to the following persons and institutions:

H.R.H. Princess Eugenie of Greece and Denmark for the letter of Empress Marie Feodorovna which was kindly translated by Mrs. Birgitta Hillingsø of Copenhagen. The Hon. Patrick Lindsay through whose good offices the surprise of the 1914 Imperial Easter Egg, the Sedan Chair Automaton from the collection of the late Sir Charles Clore, was made available by Vivien Duffield for further studies.

Dr. Geza von Habsburg-Lothringen was always generous with his experienced advice in discussing with me the various aspects of Fabergé's oeuvre, while Prince George Galitzine, London, and Countess Marie Madelaine Mordvinoff, Paris, gave me hitherto unpublished documents.

New biographical information on the workmasters and their portrait photographs are the fruits of research by Christina Ehrnroot-Ahlqvist of Tillander & Cie., Helsinki. Dr. Marina Lopato of the Hermitage, Leningrad, helped with information on material in the Russian archives. Charles Truman of the Victoria and Albert Museum, London, pointed out to me the correspondence of Oswald Jones, now in the Shrewsbury Museum.

I especially thank Madame Tatiana Fabergé of Geneva for information and documents relating to the history of the firm and am grateful as well to A. C. Fabergé of Austin, Texas.

Margaret Kelly helped with detailed information on the objects in the FORBES Magazine Collection. Alice M. Ilich of Christie's, New York, and Bianca T. Bellelli kindly corrected the manuscript, which was put in presentable form by Mary Gavot.

It is Christopher Forbes above all to whom I am grateful for initiating the concept of this work, and I am particularly appreciative of his unflagging support and enthusiasm.

A. v. S.

For the help given in the preparation of "Fabergé in Thailand," the author is indebted to the following persons: In Thailand, His Royal Highness Prince Bhanubhand Yukala, Thanpuying Suprapada Kasemsant, Dr. Kuhn Pharani Kirtiputra, Mr. Smitthi Siribhadra, and Assistant Professor Tongthong Chandransu. In Washington, D.C., Mrs. Yoopa Pranich of the Thai Support Foundation; Mrs. Katrina Taylor, Hillwood Curator; and Mrs. Paulette Betteley, Mrs. Jeannette Harper and Mrs. Sally Lilley, members of the Hillwood staff who accompanied the author on the Bangkok trip.

The historical information for this essay came from interviews with two Thai professors who had access to documents and books from the Thai archives, and from the following books:

Bunge, Frederick M., ed. *Thailand, A Country Study.* Washington, D.C.: The American University, 1980.

Thailand into the 80's. Bangkok: Office of the Prime Minister, 1979.

R. D. R. B.

Photo Credits